The Pleasantness

of a

Religious Life

Opened and Proved

by

Matthew Henry

Soli Deo Gloria Publications
...for instruction in righteousness...

Soli Deo Gloria Publications
P.O. Box 451, Morgan, PA 15064
(412) 221-1901/FAX 221-1902

*

The Pleasantness of a Religious Life
was published by Robert Carter in
New York in 1847. This reprint
by Soli Deo Gloria is 1996.
Printed in the USA.

*

ISBN 1-57358-044-9

*

The publisher acknowledges the kindness of the Speer Library at Princeton
Theological Seminary in making this
book available for reprinting.

Contents

To the Reader   3

Introduction   7

Chapter I   12

Chapter II   36

Chapter III   73

Chapter IV   104

Chapter V   121

Chapter VI   136

Chapter VII   159

TO THE READER.

THAT distinction which the learned Dr. Henry
More insists so much upon, in his explanation
of the grand mystery of godliness, between the
animal life and the divine life, is certainly of
great use to lead us into the understanding of
that mystery. What was the fall and apostacy
of man, and what is still his sin and misery,
but the soul's revolt from the divine life, and
giving up itself wholly to the animal life? And
what was the design of our Redeemer, but to
recover us to the divine and spiritual life again,
by the influences of his grace? And to this his
gospel has a direct tendency; his religion is all
spiritual and divine, while all other religions
savour of the animal life. Christianity (saith
he) is that period of the wisdom and providence
of God, wherein the animal life is remarkably
insulted, and triumphed over by the Divine.
Book II. Chap 7. And so far and no further,
are we Christians indeed, as this revolution is
brought about in our souls.

The conflict is between these two : nothing
draws more forcibly than pleasure. In order,
therefore, to the advancing of the interests of
the divine life in myself and others, I have

here endeavoured, as God has enabled me, to make it evident, that the pleasures of the divine life are unspeakably better, and more deserving, than those of the animal life; were people convinced of this, we should gain our point.

The substance of this was preached last year in six sermons, in the ordinary course of my ministry, among many other reasons why we should be religious. I was then solicited to make it public; and now take this opportunity to prepare it for the press, when, through the good hand of my God upon me, I have finished the fifth volume of my Exposition, before I go about the sixth. And herein, I confess, I indulge an inclination of my own; for this doctrine of the pleasantness of religion is what I have long had a particular kindness for, and taken all occasions to mention. Yet I would not thus far have gratified either my friends' request, or my own inclination, If I had not thought, that by the blessing of God, it might be of some service to the common interest of Christ's kingdom, and the common salvation of precious souls.

MAT. HENRY

May 31, 1741.

THE PLEASANTNESS

OF A

RELIGIOUS LIFE.

Prov. iii. 17.

HER WAYS ARE WAYS OF PLEASANTNESS,
AND ALL HER PATHS ARE PEACE

TRUE Religion is often in Scripture,
and particularly in this book of the
Proverbs, represented and recommended
to us under the name and character of
" Wisdom," because it is the highest im-
provement of human nature, and the best
and surest guide of human life. It was
one of the first and most ancient discoveries of God's mind to the children of
men. When God made a " weight for
the winds" and a " decree for the rain,"
when he brought all the other creatures

A 3

under the established rule and law of
their creation, according to their respec-
tive capacities, then he declared this to
man, a reasonable creature, as the law
of his creation,—" Behold the fear of
the Lord, that is wisdom; and to depart from evil, is understanding," Job
xxviii. 28.

The great men of the world, who en-
gross its wealth and honours, are pretenders to wisdom, and think none do so
well for themselves as they; but, though
their neighbours applaud them, and
" their posterity," who reap the fruit of
this worldly wisdom, " approve their
sayings," yet " this their way is their
folly;" and so it will appear, when God
himself shall call them " Fools," and require their souls. The learned men of
the world were well-wishers to wisdom,
and modestly called themselves " Lovers
of wisdom;" and many wise principles
we have from them, and wise precepts,
and yet their philosophy failed them in
that in which man's great duty and interest lies—acquainting himself with his
Maker, and keeping up communion with

him; herein they that "professed themselves to be wise, became fools," and "the world by wisdom knew not God."

But true Christians are, without doubt, the truly wise men. They understand themselves best, and on which side their interest lies, who give up themselves to the conduct of Christ and his word and Spirit; who consult his oracles and govern themselves by them, which are indeed the true oracles of reason. Men never begin to be wise till they begin to be religious; and they then leave off to be wise, when they leave off to do good.

Now, to recommend to us the study and practice of this true wisdom, to bring us into a willing subjection to her authority, and to keep us to a conscientious observance of her dictates, the great God is here, by Solomon, reasoning with us, from those topics which, in other cases, are usually cogent and commanding enough. Interest is the great governess of the world. Every one is for what he can get, and therefore applies himself to that which he thinks he can

get by. The common inquiry is, " Who
will shew us any good ?" We would all
be happy, would all be easy.

Now it is here demonstrated by eternal Truth itself, that it is our interest
to be religious; and therefore religion
deserves to be called wisdom, because it
teaches us to do well for ourselves. And
it is certain, that the way to be happy,
that is, perfectly holy hereafter, is to
be holy, that is, truly happy now. It
is laid down for a principle here, " Happy is the man that findeth wisdom," that
finds the principles and habits of it planted in his own soul by divine grace ; that,
having diligently sought, has at length
found, that " pearl of great price."

This is that which the text speaks of.
We are here assured, that the ways of
religion are ways of pleasantness; not
only pleasant ways, but " ways of pleasantness ;" as if pleasantness were confined to those ways, and not to be found
any where else ; and as if the pleasantness arose not from any foreign circum-
stance, but from the innate goodness of
the ways themselves. Or it denotes the

superlative pleasantness of religion; it is as pleasant as pleasantness itself.

Wisdom's ways are so, that is, the ways which she has directed us to walk in, the ways of her commandments. They are such, that if we keep close to them, and go on in them, we shall certainly find true pleasure and satisfaction.

It is added that "all her paths are peace." Peace is sometimes put for all good; here some take it for the good of safety and protection. Many ways are pleasant; they are clean, and look smooth: but they are dangerous, either not sound at bottom, or beset with thieves: but the ways of wisdom have in them a holy security, as well as a holy serenity; and they that walk in them, have God himself for their "shield," as well as their "sun," and are not only joyful in the hope of good, but are, or may be "quiet" also "from the fear of evil." But we may take it for the good of pleasure and delight; and so it imports the same as the former part of the verse. As there is "pleasantness" in wisdom's ways, so there is "peace" in all her paths.

There is not only peace in the end of religion, but peace in the way. There is not only peace provided as a bed, for good men to lie down in at night, when their work is done, and their warfare is accomplished; but there is also peace provided as a shade, for good men to work in all day, that they may not only do their work, but do it with delight; for even the " work of righteousness," as well as its reward, " shall be peace;" and the immediate " effect of righteousness," as well as its issue at last, " quietness and assurance for ever," Isaiah xxxii. 17.

There is not only this peace in the way of religion in general, but in the particular " paths" of that way. View it in the several acts and instances of it, in the exercise of every grace, in the performance of every duty, and you will find that what is said of the body of Christianity, is true of every part of it —it is peace. Look into all the paths of wisdom, make trial of them all, and you will find there are none to be excepted, none to be quarrelled with. They are all uniform, and of a piece. The same golden thread of peace and pleasure runs through the whole web of serious godliness.

We cannot say so of this world, that all its paths are peace, however some of them may pretend to give the mind a little satisfaction. Its pleasures have their alloys. That which one thing sweetens, another comes presently and embitters. But as there is a universal rectitude in the principles of religion, as " all its precepts concerning all things are right;" so there is an universal peace and pleasure in the practice of religion. All our paths, if such as they should be, will be such as we could wish.

The doctrine, therefore, contained in these words, is this—true piety has true pleasure in it ; or thus—the ways of religion are pleasant and peaceful ways.

CHAPTER I.

THE EXPLICATION OF THE DOCTRINE.

IT is a plain truth which we have here laid down, and there is little in it that needs explication. It were well for us, if we would but as readily subscribe to the certainty of it, as we apprehend the sense and meaning of it. Nor will any complain that it is hard to be understood, but those who know no other pleasures than those of sense, and relish no other, and therefore resolve not to give credit to it. Those who think, 'How can this be, that there should be pleasure in piety?' will be ready to ask, 'What is the meaning of this doctrine?' and to call it a 'hard saying.'

You know what pleasure is. I hope you know, in some degree, what the pleasure of the mind is, a pleasure which the soul has the sensation of. And do

you not know, in some degree, what
piety is, a due regard to a God above
us, and having the eyes of the soul ever
lifted up unto him? Then you know
what I mean when I say, that there is
an abundance of real pleasure and satisfaction in the ways of religion and godliness.

I. But to help you a little in the understanding of it, and to prevent mistakes, observe, first, that I speak of true
piety, and of that as far as it goes.

1. Hypocrites are very much strangers to the delights and pleasures of religion; nay, they are altogether so, for
it is joy which those strangers do not
intermeddle with. Counterfeit piety
can never bring in true pleasure. He
that acts a part upon a stage, though it
be the part of one that is ever so pleasant, though he may exhibit the pleasantness well, does not experience it.
The pleasures of God's house lie not
in the outer court, but within the veil.
None know what the " peace of God"
means, but those who are under the dominion and operation of his grace; nor

can any that " deny the power of godliness," expect to share in the pleasures of it. " When wisdom enters into thine heart," takes possession of that, and becomes a living, active principle there, then, and not till then, it is " pleasant unto thy soul," Prov. ii. 10. They who aim at no more than the credit of religion before men, justly fall short of the comfort of it in themselves.

Hypocrites have other things that they delight in—the satisfactions of the world, the gratifications of sense; and these put their mouths out of taste for spiritual pleasures, so that they have no pleasure in them. They who have their hearts upon the marketings, are weary of the " new moons" and the " sabbaths," Amos viii. 5. With good reason therefore does Job ask, " Will the hypocrite delight himself in the Almighty?" No; his soul takes its ease in the creature, and returns not to the Creator as its rest and home.

Some transitory pleasure a hypocrite may have in religion, from a land-flood of sensible affections, who yet has not the least taste of the "river of God's pleasures." There were those who "delighted to know God's ways;" they met with some agreeable notions in them, which surprised them and pleased their fancies, but they did not delight to walk in them. The stony ground "received the word with joy," and yet received no lasting benefit by it. Herod "heard John gladly." He found something very agreeable in his sermons, and something which natural conscience could not but embrace, and yet he could not bear to be reproved for his Herodias. A florid preacher, such as Ezekiel was, may be as "a very lovely song of one that can play well on an instrument," and yet, at the same time, the word of the Lord, if it touch the conscience, and shew the people their transgressions, is to them a reproach.

They whose hearts are not right with God in their religion, cannot have the pleasures of communion with God; for it is the soul only that converses with

God. " Bodily exercise profiteth little," and therefore pleases little. The service of God is a burden and a task to an un- sanctified, unrenewed heart; it is out of its element when it is brought into that air. Nor can they take any pleasure in communing with their own consciences, or in their own reflections; for they are ready, upon all occasions, to give them uneasiness by charging them with that which is disagreeable to their profession, and gives the lie to it. And though they cry " peace, peace," to themselves, they have that within them, which tells them that the God of heaven does not speak " peace" to them ; and this casts a damp upon all their pleasures ; so that their religion itself gives them pain; God himself is a terror to them; and the gospel itself condemns them for their insincerity. In time of trouble and dis- tress none are so much afraid as the " sinners in Zion," the secret sinners there ; and fearfulness is the greatest surprise of all to the hypocrites that were at " ease in Zion," and thought its strong-holds would be their security,

Amos vi. 1. And therefore it is that hypocrites cast off religion, and discharge themselves of the professions of it, after they have awhile disguised themselves with it, because it does not sit easy; and they are weary of it. Tradesmen who take no pleasure in their business, will not stick to it long; no more will they who take no pleasure in their religion: nor will anything carry us through the outward difficulties of it, but the inward delights of it; if these be wanting, the tree is not watered, and therefore even " its leaf" will soon " wither." The hypocrite will not always call upon God—will not long do it, because he " will not delight himself in the Almighty." This ought not to be a stumbling-block to us. Hypocrites in religion prove apostates from it; the reason is, because they never found it pleasant; they never found it pleasant, because they were never sincere in it, which was their fault, and not the fault of the religion they professed.

Let us therefore take heed, and beware of hypocrisy, if ever we hope to find pleasure in religion. Counterfeit piety has some other end in view—some other end to serve than that which is the spring of true delight. They who rest in that, " hew them out cisterns" that can hold but little water, and that dead water ; nay, " broken cisterns that can hold no water ;" and how can they expect the pleasure which they have, who cleave to, and continually draw from the " Fountain of life" and " living waters ?" No ; as their principles are, such are their pleasures ; as their aims are, such are their joys ; they appeal to the world, and to the world they shall go. But let not the credit of religion suffer for the sake of those who are only pretenders to it, and indeed enemies to it.

2. It is possible that true Christians may, through their own fault and folly, want very much of the pleasure of religion ; and therefore, I say, true piety, as far as it goes, is very pleasant ; as far as it has its due influence upon us, and is rightly understood and lived up to.

We abide by it, that Wisdom's ways are always pleasant, and yet we must own that Wisdom's children are sometimes unpleasant, and therein come short of justifying Wisdom in this matter as they ought to do, and rather give advantage to her accusers and prejudice to her cause. Either they miss these ways, and turn aside out of them, and so lose the pleasure that is to be found in them ; or they refuse to take the comfort which they might have in these ways. They hamper themselves with needless perplexities, make the yoke heavy which Christ has made easy, and that frightful which he designed should be encouraging. They indulge themselves, and then, as Jonah when he was angry, justify themselves in causeless griefs and fears, and think they do well to put themselves into an agony, to be very heavy and sore amazed, and their souls exceeding sorrowful.

But let not true piety suffer in its reputation because of this ; for though it be called a religious melancholy, it is not so, for it is contrary to the very na-

ture and design of religion, while it
shelters itself under the colour of it, and
pretends to take rise from it. It is rather to be called a superstitious melancholy, arising from such a slavish fear
of God as the heathens were driven to
by their dæmons and barbarous sacrifices; and there is a great injury to the
honour of his goodness, as well as a
great injury to themselves.

If the professors of religion look for
that in the world, which is to be had in
God only, and that is perfect happiness;
or if they look for that in themselves,
which is to be had in Christ only, and
that is a perfect righteousness; or if
they look for that on earth, which is to
be had in heaven only, and that is perfect holiness; and then fret, and grieve,
and go mourning from day to day, because they are disappointed in their expectations, they may thank themselves;
"Why seek they the living among the
dead ?"

Let but religion, true and pure religion, in all the laws and instances of it,
command and prevail, and these tears

will soon be wiped away. Let but God's
servants take their work before them,
allow each principle of their religion its
due weight, and each practice of it its
due place and proportion; and let them
not dash one precept of the gospel,
any more than one table of the law, in
pieces against the other; let them look
upon it to be as much their duty to rejoice in Christ Jesus, as to mourn for
sin; nay, and more, for this mourning
is in order to that joy; and then we
shall not fear that their sorrows will,
in the least, shake the truth of our doctrine, for as far as religion is carried, it
will carry this character along with it,
and farther it cannot be expected.

II. In true piety, I say, there is a
pleasure; there is that which we may
find comfort in, and fetch satisfaction
from. There is a pleasant good, as well
as an useful one. That is pleasant which
is agreeable, which the soul rejoices in,
or, at least, reposes in; which it relish-
es, pleases itself with, and desires the
continuance and repetition of. Let a
man's faculties be in their due frame

and temper, not vitiated, corrupted, or
depraved, and there is that in the exercise of religion, which highly suits them,
and satisfies them.   And this pleasure is
such as is not alloyed with anything to
cast a damp upon it.

1. The ways of religion are right and
pleasant; they are pleasant without the
alloy of injury and iniquity.   Sin pretends to have its pleasures, but they are
the " perverting of that which is right;"
they are " stolen waters," unjust, though
pleasant; but the pleasures of godliness
are as agreeable to the rectitude of our
nature, as they are gratifying to the
pure and undebauched desires of it.   It
is " the way in which we should go;"
and the way in which, if we were not
wretchedly degenerated, we would go
of choice.

They are right, for they are marked
out to us by our rightful Lord, who
having given us the being of rational
creatures, has authority to give us a law
suited to our being; and he has done it,
both by natural conscience, and by the
written word.   He has said, " This is

the way, walk ye in it." It is not only permitted and allowed us, but charged and commanded us, to walk in it. He has sent us, as messengers from him, to travel this road upon his errand.

They are right, for they lead directly to our great end; they have a tendency to our welfare here and for ever. They are the only right way to that which is the felicity of our being; which we shall certainly miss and come short of, if we do not walk in this way.

But that is not all; they are also pleasant: "Behold how good and how pleasant!" It is the hapiness of those who fear God, that he not only "teaches them in the way that he shall choose," but also that "their souls shall dwell at ease." Justly may they dwell at ease, who have infinite Wisdom itself to choose their way, and to guide them in it. That may be right which is not pleasant, and that pleasant which is not right; but religion is both: therefore in the next verse it is compared to the tree of life. The tree of knowledge was indeed "pleasant to the eyes," and a

"tree to be desired," but it was forbidden ; and therefore religion is called a
"tree of life," which was not only pleasant, but was allowed till sin entered.

2. They are easy and pleasant; pleasant without the alloy of toil and difficulty, any more than what arises from
the corruption of our own nature.
That indeed makes such opposition, that
we have need of arguments to prove
the practice of religion easy : but it is
more than this, it is pleasant.

Much less is said than is intended,
when we are told that "his commandments are not grievous." They are not
only not grievous and galling, but they
are gracious and pleasing. His yoke is
"easy." The word there used, signifies more than easy; it is sweet and
gentle ; not only easy as a yoke is to
the neck, when it is so well fitted as not
to hurt it, but easy as a pillow is to the
head when the head is weary and sleepy.
It is not only tolerable, but very comfortable. There is not only no matter
of complaint in the way of God, nothing to hurt us, but there is abundant

matter of joy and rejoicing. It is not only work which is not weariness, but work which is its own wages; such a tree of life as will not only screen us from the storm and tempest, and feed us with necessary food, but we may " sit under the shadow of it with great delight, and the fruit of it will be sweet unto our taste."

3. They are gainful and pleasant, and have not the alloy of expense and loss. That may be profitable, which yet may be unpleasant, and that unpleasant which afterward may prove very unprofitable and prejudicial. But religion brings both pleasure with it, and profit after it. The pleasures of religion do not cost us dear; there is no loss by them when the account comes to be balanced. The gain of this world is usually fetched in by toil and uneasy labour, which are grievous to flesh and blood. The servants of this world are drudges to it; " they rise up early, sit up late," and " eat the bread of sorrows," in pursuit of its wealth; they labour, and bereave their souls of good. But the

servants of God have a pleasure even in the work they are to get by, and which they shall be recompensed for. Beside the tendency that there is in the practice of serious godliness to our happiness in the other life, there is much in it that conduces to our comfort in this life. David observes, to the honour of religion, that not only after keeping, but "in keeping God's commandments there is a great reward ;" a present great reward of obedience in obedience. "A good man is satisfied from himself," that is, from that which divine grace has wrought in him ; and the saints are said to "sing in the ways of the Lord," as those that find them pleasant ways.

The more closely we adhere to the rules of religion, the more intimate our converse is with divine things ; and the more we live with an eye to Christ and another world, the more comfort we are likely to have in our own bosoms. "Great peace have they that love God's law," and the more they love it the greater their peace is ; nay, it is promised to the church, that " all her chil-

dren shall be taught of the Lord," and
then "great shall be the peace of her
children;" it shall be entailed upon
them—"peace like a river," rolling on
from age to age.

III. I call it a true pleasure. As
there is science falsely so called, so there
is pleasure falsely so called. But this
we are sure of, that it is a true pleasure
which religion secures to us; a pleasure
that deserves the name and answers it to
the full.

1. It is a true pleasure, for it is real
and not counterfeit. Carnal worldlings
pretend a great satisfaction in the enjoyments of the world and the gratifications
of sense. "Soul, take thine ease," says
one; "I have found me out substance,"
says another, even "the life of my
hand." "The wicked boasts of his heart's
desire;" but Solomon assures us, not
only that the "end of that mirth is
heaviness," but that even in "laughter
the heart is sorrowful." Both those
that make a God of their belly, and those
that make a God of their money, find
such a constant pain and uneasiness at-

tending their spiritual idolatries, that
their pleasure is but from the teeth outward. Discontent at present disappoint-
ments, and the fear of worse ; ungoverned passions, which seldom are made less
turbulent by the gratifications of the
appetite; and above all, conscience of
guilt and dread of divine wrath—these
give them the lie when they boast of
their pleasu res, which, with such alloys,
are not to be boasted of. They would
not be thought to be disappointed in
that which they have chosen for their
happiness, and therefore they seem to be
pleased when really their heart cannot
but "know its own bitterness."

And many of the good things of this
world, of which we said, ' these same
shall comfort us,' prove vexatious to us ;
and we are disappointed in that, wherein
we most promised ourselves satisfaction.
" If we say, our bed shall comfort us,"
perhaps it is not a bed to rest on, but a
bed to toss on, as it was to poor Job,
when " wearisome nights were appointed to him." Nay, such strangers are we
to real pleasure in the things of this life,

and so often do we deceive ourselves
with that which is counterfeit, that we
wish to live to those days of life which
we are told will be "evil days," and
those years of which we are assured that
we shall say, "We have no pleasure
in them."

But the pleasures of religion are solid,
substantial pleasures, and not painted;
gold, and not gilded over. These sons
of pleasure "inherit substance." It is
that which is the firm foundation, the
strong superstructure, the "consolations
of God, which are neither few nor
small;" while a vain and foolish world
"cause their eyes to fly upon that which
is not." Worldly people pretend to the
joy they have not; but godly people
conceal the joy they have. They have,
like their Master, "meat to eat which
the world knows not of."

2. It is rational, and not brutish. It
is the pleasure of the soul, not of sense;
it is the peculiar pleasure of a man, not
that which we have in common with
the inferior creatures. The pleasures of
religion are not those of the mere animal

life, which arise from the gratification of the senses of the body and its appetites ; no, they affect the soul, that part of us by which we are allied to the world of spirits, that noble part of us ; and therefore are to be called the true pleasures of a man.

The brute creatures have the same pleasures of sense that we have, and perhaps, in some of them, the senses are more exquisite, and consequently they have them in a much higher degree ; nor are their pleasures liable to the correctives of reason and conscience, as ours are. Who live such merry lives as the Leviathan, who " plays in the deep," or as the birds that " sing among the branches ?"

But what are these to a man, who, being " taught more than the beasts of the earth, and made wiser than the fowls of heaven," and being dignified above the beasts, not so much by the powers of reason, as by a capacity for religion, is certainly designed for enjoyments of a more excellent nature ; for spiritual and heavenly delights ? When God

made man, he left him not to the enjoyments of the wide world with the
other creatures, but enclosed him in a
paradise, a garden of pleasures, where he
should have delights proper for him ;
signified indeed by the pleasures of a
garden, pleasant trees, and their fruits,
but really the delights of a soul which
was a ray of divine light, and a spark of
divine fire newly breathed into him from
above, and on which God's image and
likeness were imprinted. And we never
recover the felicity, which we lost by
our first parents' indulging the appetite
of the body, till we come to the due
relish of those pleasures which man has
in common with angels, and a due contempt of those which he has in common
with the brutes.

The pleasures of Wisdom's ways may
at second-hand affect the body, and be
an advantage to that ; hence it is said to
be " health to the navel," and " marrow
to the bones ;" but its residence is in the
" hidden man of the heart," and its comforts " delight the soul in the multitude
of its thoughts." It is pleasant to the

soul, and makes it like a watered garden. These are pleasures which a man, by the assistance of divine grace, may reason himself into, and not, as it is with sensual pleasures, reason himself out of.

There is no pleasure separate from that of religion, which pretends to be an intellectual pleasure, except that of learning and that of honour; but as to the pleasure of a proud man in his dignities, and the respects paid him in the acclamations of a crowd, it does but affect the fancy. It is vain-glory, it is not glory. It is but the folly of him that receives the honour, fed by the folly of them that gave it. So that it does not deserve to be called a rational pleasure. It is a lust of the mind that is gratified by it, and that is as much an instance of our degeneracy as any of the lusts of the flesh are.

And as to the pleasures of a scholar, abstracted from religion, it is indeed rational and intellectual; but it is only the pleasure of the mind in knowing truth, and not its enjoying good. Solomon, who had as much of this pleasure as ever any man had, and as nice a taste for it, yet has assured us from his own experienee, that in " much wisdom" of this kind is " much grief," and " he that increaseth knowledge increaseth sorrow." But the pleasures which the holy soul has in knowing God and in communion with him, are not only of a spiritual nature, but they are satisfying ; they fill the soul, and make a happiness adequate to its best affections.

3. It is durable, and not flashy and transitory. That is true pleasure, which will continue with us as a " tree of life," and not wither as the " green herb ;" which will be, not as the light of a candle, which is soon burnt out, but as that of the sun, which is a faithful witness in heaven. We reckon that most valuable, which is most durable.

The pleasures of sense are fading and perishing ; as the " world passeth away," so do " the lusts of it ;" that which at first pleases and satisfies, after a while palls and surfeits. " As the crackling of thorns under a pot," which makes a great blaze and a great noise for a little

c

while, but soon ends in soot and ashes, such is the "laughter of the fool," the "end of his mirth is heaviness." But the pleasures of religion will abide. They wither not in the winter, nor tarnish with time, nor does age wrinkle their beauty. Frosts nip them not, nor do storms blast them. They continue through the greatest opposition of events, and despise that time and "chance" which "happens to all things under the sun." Believers, when they are sorrowful, are but "as sorrowful," for they are "always rejoicing." If an immortal soul make an eternal God its chief joy, what should hinder, but that it should "rejoice evermore?" for as the treasure, so the pleasure, is laid up there, where "neither moth nor rust can corrupt, nor thieves break through and steal." The joy which Christ gives to those that are his, is joy which "no man taketh from them;" it is their heart that rejoices. Their joys are the beginning of everlasting pleasures, the earnests and foretastes of them; so that they are in effect, "pleasures for evermore."

The great truth, then, which I desire my heart and yours may be fully convinced of, is this ;—a holy, heavenly life, spent in the service of God, in communion with him, is, without doubt, the most pleasant and comfortable life any man can live in this world.

CHAPTER II.

THE PLEASURE OF BEING RELIGIOUS, PROVED FROM THE NATURE OF TRUE RELIGION, AND MANY PARTICULAR INSTANCES OF IT.

THE doctrine needs no further explanation, nor can have any better, than our own experience of it ; but the chief part of this undertaking is to prove the truth of it. And O that God would set it before us in a true light, so that we may be all convinced of it, and embrace it as a faithful saying and well worthy of all acceptation, that a godly life is a pleasant life ; and that we may be wrought upon to live such a life!

Pleasure is a tempting thing. What yields delight cannot but attract desire. Surely, if we were but fully persuaded of this, that religion has pleasure on its side, we should be wrought upon by the allurement of it to be religious. It is certainly so; let us not be in doubt of it. Here is a bait that has no hook under it, a pleasure courting you which has no pain attending it, no bitterness at the latter end of it; a pleasure which God himself invites you to, and which will make you happy, truly and eternally happy; and shall not this work upon you?

To make way for the proof of it, I would only desire two things;—first, that you would lay aside prejudice, and give a fair and impartial hearing to this cause, and not prejudge it. He that answers any matter before he hears it out, it is "folly and shame" to him; especially if it be matter of great importance and concern to himself, a matter of life and death. Be willing, therefore, to believe, that it is possible there may be, and then I doubt not but to make out that it is certain there is, true pleasure in true religion.

You have a notion, it may be, and are confirmed in it by the common cry of the multitude, that religion is a sour, melancholy thing; that it is to bid farewell to all pleasure and delight, and to spend your days in grief, and your years in sighing; and if we offer any thing to the contrary, and tell you that it is a pleasant thing, and the best entertainment that can be to the mind, you are ready to say, as Ezekiel's hearers did of him, " Doth he not speak parables?" Does he not speak paradoxes? You startle at it, and start from it as a hard saying. As Nathaniel said, "Can any good thing come out of Nazareth?" so you are ready to say, " Can there be any pleasure in religion?" Believe it, there can be, there cannot but be, pleasure in it.

Do not measure religion by the follies of some who profess it, but do not live up to their profession, nor adorn it: let them bear their own burden, or clear themselves as they can; but you are to judge of things, not persons, and therefore ought not to be prejudiced against religion for their sakes. Nor should you measure it by the ill opinions which its adversaries have of it, or the ill name which they endeavour to put on it, who neither know it, nor love it, and therefore care not what unjust things they say to justify themselves in the contempt of it, and to hinder others from embracing it; but think freely of this matter.

I desire, secondly, that you would admit this as a principle, and abide by it—that the soul is the man. This is the postulatum that I lay down, in order to the proof of the doctrine ; and I hope it will be readily granted me, that man is principally to be considered as an intellectual, immortal being, endued with spiritual powers and capacities, allied to the world of spirits ; that there is a spirit in man, which has sensations and dispositions of its own, active and receptive faculties, distinct from those of the body : and that this is the part of us, which we are, and ought to be most concerned about ; because it is really well or ill with us, according as it is well or ill with our souls. Believe, that in man's present state, the soul and the body have separate and contesting interests; the body thinks it is its interest to have its appetites gratified, and to be indulged in its pleasures; while the soul knows it is its interest to have the appetites of the body subdued and mortified, that spiritual pleasures may be the better relished; and we are here upon our trial, which of these two we will side with. Be wise, therefore; be resolute, and shew yourselves men who are actuated and governed by reason, and are affected with things as reason represents them to you: not reason as it is in the mere natural man, clouded, and plunged, and lost in sense; but reason elevated and guided by divine revelation to us, and divine grace in us. Walk by faith, and not by sense. Let the God that made you, and knows you, and wishes you well, and from whom your judgment must proceed, determine your sentiments in this matter, and the work is done.

Now I shall, in the first place, endeavour to prove this doctrine, by shewing you what religion is, wherein it consists

and what those things are which con-
stitute serious godliness; and then you
shall yourselves judge, whether it be
not in its own nature pleasant. If you
understand religion aright, you will find
that it has an innate sweetness in it, in-
separable from it. Let it but speak for
itself, and it will recommend itself. The
very exhibition of it in its own features
and proportions, is enough to bring us
all in love with it.

You may see the pleasure of religion
in twelve instances of it.

I. To be religious is "to know the
only true God, and Jesus Christ whom
he hath sent." And is not this pleasant?
This is the first thing we have to do, to
get our understandings rightly informed
concerning both the object and the me-
dium of our religious regards, to seek
and to receive this light from heaven,
to have it diffused through our souls as
the morning light in the air, and to be
turned to the impressions of it, " as the
clay to the seal;" and this is a pleasure
to the soul that understands itself, and
its own true interest. " Truly the light

is sweet, and a pleasant thing it is for
the eyes to behold the sun;" " it rejoic-
eth the heart." Hence light is often
put for joy and comfort; but no light
is comparable to that of "the knowledge of the glory of God in the face of
Jesus Christ." This is finding the
knowledge we had lost, and must for
ever have despaired of finding, if God
had not made it known to us by the
Spirit. It is finding the knowledge
that we are undone without, and happy
for ever in; for what is heaven but this
knowledge in perfection? It is finding
the knowledge which the soul would
covet and rest in, if it had but recovered
itself from the delirium, which by the
fall it is thrown into. They that " sat
in darkness," when they begin to be religious, begin to "see a great light."
It is a pleasing surprise to them: it is
coming into a new world; such a pleasure as none could know so well, as he
that had his sight given him, though he
was "born blind." " Blessed are your
eyes, says Christ to those whom he
had brought into an acquaintance with

himself, " for they see." " Apply thy heart to my knowledge," says Solomon, " for it is a pleasant thing if thou keep it within thee." Thou wilt " eat honey because it is good, and the honeycomb which is sweet to the taste; so shall the knowledge of wisdom be to thy soul." Could a learned man, that had hit upon a demonstration in mathematics, cry out in a transport of joy, " I have found it,—I have found it;" and may not they much more boast of their discovery, who have found the knowledge of the Most High?

There is no pleasure in any learning like that of learning Christ, and the things that belong to our everlasting peace; for that which is known is not small and trivial, is not doubtful and uncertain, is not foreign to us, and which we are not concerned in; but it is great and sure, and of the last importance to us, and the knowledge of it gives us satisfaction. Here we may rest our souls. To know the perfections of the divine nature, the unsearchable riches of divine grace; to be led into the mystery of our

redemption and reconciliation by Christ
—this is food ; such knowledge as this
is a feast to the soul : it is meat ·indeed
and drink indeed, it is the knowledge of
that " which the angels desire to look
into." If the knowledge of the law of
God was so sweet to David, " sweeter
than honey to his taste," how much
more should the knowledge of the gospel
of Christ be so to us !

II. To be religious is to return to God,
and repose in him as the rest of our·souls.
And is not this pleasant ? It is not only
for our understandings to embrace the
knowledge of him, but our affections to
fasten upon the enjoyment of him. It
is to love God as our chief good, and to
rest in that love ; to " love him with all
our heart, and soul, and mind, and
strength," who is well worthy of all
that love, and infinitely more ; amiable
in himself, gracious to us ; who will accept our love, and return it ; who has
promised to " love those that love him."
The love of God reigning in the soul
(and that is true religion) is as much a
satisfaction to the soul, as the love of

the world is a vexation to it, when it comes to be reflected upon, and is found to be so ill bestowed. How pleasant must it needs be, so far to recover ourselves, as to quit the world for a portion and happiness, and to depend upon him to be so, who has enough in him to answer our utmost expectations!—when we have in vain sought for satisfaction where it is not to be had, to seek it and find it where it is!—to come from doating upon " lying vanities," and " spending our money for that which is not bread," to live, and live plentifully, upon a God that is enough, a God all-sufficient: and in him to enjoy " our own mercies!" Did ever any thing speak a mind more easy and better pleased than that saying of David, " Return unto thy rest, O my soul!" to God as thy rest, for in him I am where I would be, I have what I would have! or this, " O my soul, thou hast said unto the Lord, thou art my Lord; the portion of my inheritance, and of my cup." And then again, " the lines are fallen to me in pleasant places, and I have a goodly heritage ;" or this, " whom have I in heaven but thee, and there is none upon earth that I desire in comparison of thee ; for when flesh and heart fail, thou art the strength" and joy " of my heart; and my portion for ever." Psalm lxxiii. 25, 26.

Religion consists not in raptures and transports ; yet, without doubt, holy souls that are at home in God, that have " made the Most High their habitation," whose desires are toward him, whose delights are in him, who are in him as their centre and element, " dwell at ease." None can imagine the pleasure that a believer has in his covenant-relation to God, and interest in him, and the assurance of his love. Have I taken " thy testimonies" to be " my heritage for ever ?" surely they are the " rejoicing of my heart ;" I cannot be better provided for. When King Asa brought his people to renew their covenant with God, it is said, " they sware unto the Lord with a loud voice, and with shoutings, and with trumpets," 2 Chron. xv. 14, 15. " And all Judah rejoiced at

the oath, for they had sworn with all
their heart." When we come to make
it our own act and deed, to join ourselves to the Lord in an everlasting covenant, and are upright with him in it,
we cannot but be pleased with what we
have done. It is a marriage covenant;
it is made with joy; " My beloved is
mine, and I am his."

III. To be religious is to come to God
as a Father, in and by Jesus Christ as a
Mediator. And is not this pleasant?
We have not only the pleasure of knowing and loving God, but the pleasure of
drawing nigh to him, and having by
faith an humble freedom and intimacy
with him. " Blessed are they that dwell
in his courts! They shall be satisfied
with the goodness of his house, even of
his holy temple."

Religion is described by coming to
God; and what can be more agreeable
to a soul that comes from him? It is
to come to God as a child to his father,
to his father's house, to his father's arms,
and to cry, " Abba, Father." To come
as a petitioner to his prince, is a privi-

lege; but to come as a child to his father is a pleasure: and this pleasure have all the saints who have received the "spirit of adoption." They can look up to the God that made them, as one that loves them, and has a tender compassion for them, as a father has for his children, and delights to do them good, taking pleasure in their prosperity; as one who, though they have offended him, is yet reconciled to them, owns them as his children, and encourages them to call him Father. When he afflicts them, they know it is in love, and for their benefit, and that still it is "their Father's good pleasure to give them the kingdom."

But this is not all. It is not only to come to God as a Father who himself loves us, but it is to come to him in the name of Jesus Christ, who is our "Advocate with the Father;" that by these "two immutable things we might have strong consolation," that we have not only a God to go to, but an Advocate to introduce us to him and speak for us. Believing in Christ is sometimes express-

ed by rejoicing in him; for it is a complacency of soul in the methods which
infinite wisdom has taken, of bringing
God and man together by a Mediator.
"We are the circumcision that rejoice
in Jesus Christ," not only rely upon him,
but triumph in him. Paul is not only
not ashamed of the cross of Christ, but
he glories in it. And when the eunuch
is brought to "believe in Christ with
all his heart," he "goes on his way rejoicing," highly pleased with what he
has done.

What a pleasure, what a satisfaction
is it, to lodge the great concerns of our
souls and eternity in such a skilful faithful hand as that of our Lord Jesus!
to cast the burden upon him who is
"able to save to the uttermost," and as
willing as he is able, and thus to make
ourselves easy! How is blessed Paul
elevated at the thought of this! "Who
is he that condemneth? it is Christ that
died, yea rather, that is risen again."
And with what pleasure does he reflect
upon the confidence he had put in Jesus
Christ! I know whom I have believed,

and am persuaded that he is able to keep that which I have committed to him against that day." They that know what it is to be in pain for sin, and in care to obtain the favour of God, cannot but know what a pleasure it is to believe in Christ as the propitiation for our sins, and our intercessor with God. How can we live a more pleasant life, than to " live by the faith of the Son of God ;" to be continually depending on him, and deriving from him, and referring all to him ; and, as we have received him, so to " walk in him ?" It is in " believing," that we are " filled with joy and peace."

IV. To be religious is to enjoy God in all our creature comforts. And is not that pleasant? It is to take the common supports and conveniences of life, be they of the richest or be they of the meanest kind, as the products of his providential care concerning us, and the gifts of his bounty to us; and in them to " taste and see that the Lord is good," good to all, good to us. It is to look above second causes to the first cause, through the creature to the Creator, and to say concerning everything which is agreeable and serviceable to us, " This I asked, and this I have from the hand of my heavenly Father." What a noble taste and relish does this put into all the blessings with which we are daily loaded, our health and ease, our rest and sleep, our food and raiment, all the satisfaction we have in our relations, peace in our dwellings, success in our callings! The sweetness of these is more than doubled, it is highly raised, when by our religion we are enabled to see them all coming to us from the goodness of God, our great benefactor, and thus to enjoy them richly ; while those who look no further than the creature, enjoy them very poorly, and only as the inferior creatures do.

Carnal, irreligious people, though they take a greater liberty in the use of the delights of sense than good people dare take, and therein think they have the advantage of them, yet they have not half the true delight in them that good people have ; not only because all excesses are a force upon nature, and surfeits are as painful as hunger and thirst, but because they deprive themselves of the comfort of receiving them from their Father's hand, and are not affected to him as obedient children. They make use of the creature, but " they have not looked unto the Maker thereof, nor had respect to him that fashioned it long ago," as good people do; and so they come short of the pleasure which good people have.

Is it not pleasant to taste covenant love in common mercies? very pleasant to see the hand of our heavenly Father spreading our table, filling our cup, making our houses safe, and our beds easy? This they do, who by faith have their eyes ever towards the Lord, who by prayer fetch in his blessing upon all their enjoyments, and by praise give the glory of them to that mercy of his which " endureth for ever." And when a continual regard is thus had to that mercy, an abundant sweetness is thereby infused into all the comforts of this life ; for as the wrath and curse of God is " the wormwood and the gall" in all

the afflictions and miseries, so his loving-kindness is the honey and oil in all
the comforts and enjoyments of this life.
It is this which is " better than life," and
which is abundantly satisfying ; which
" puts gladness into the heart, beyond
the joy of harvest." Then the " nations
are glad and sing for joy," when not only
" the earth yields her increase," but with
it "God, even their own God, gives them
his blessing." And when the church is
brought to such a sense of God's grace
as to cry out, " How great is his goodness, and how great is his beauty!" it
follows, that then " corn shall make the
young men cheerful ;" intimating that
we have no joy of them, till we are led
by these streams to the fountain, Zech.
ix. 17.

V. To be religious is to cast all our
cares upon God, and to commit all our
ways and works to him, with an assurance that " he will care for us." And is
not this pleasant ? It is a very sensible
pleasure to be eased of some pressing
burden which we are ready to sink
under ; and care is such a burden ; it is

a heaviness in the heart of man, which makes it to stoop. Now true religion enables us to " acknowledge God in all our ways," and then to depend upon him to direct our steps, and to follow his directions, not leaning to our own understanding. It is to refer ourselves, and the disposal of everything that concerns us in this world, to God, and to his will and wisdom, with an entire acquiescence in his award and arbitration. " Here I am, let the Lord do with me as seemeth good in his eyes."

To be truly godly is to have our wills melted into the will of God in everything, and to say " amen" to it, not only as a prayer, but as a covenant. It is to be fully reconciled to all the disposals of the divine providence and methods of divine grace, both concerning others and ourselves ; to be satisfied that all is well that God does, and will appear so at last, when the mystery of God shall be finished. And how does the mind enjoy itself that is come to this! How easy is it ! It is not only freed from racking anxieties, but filled with pleasing prospects:

fears are hereby silenced, and hopes
kept up and elevated. Nothing can
come amiss to those who have thus been
taught by the principles of their religion
to make the best of that which is,
because it is the will of God ; and this
is making a virtue of necessity. What
uncomfortable lives do they live, who
are continually fretting at that which
cannot be helped, quarrelling with the
disposals of Providence, when they cannot alter them ; and thus by contracting
guilt, as well as by indulging grief,
doubling every burden ! But how pleasantly do they travel through the wilderness of this world, who constantly
follow the pillar of cloud and fire, and
accommodate themselves to their lot,
whatever it is ! who, like Paul, through
Christ strengthening them, have learned in every state to be content, " knowing how to want and how to abound !"

VI. To be religious is to " rejoice in
the Lord always." And is not this pleasant ? It is not only one of the privileges
of our religion that we may rejoice, but
it is made one of the duties of it. We

are defective in our religion, if we do not live a life of complacency in God, in his being, his attributes, and his relation to us. It should be a constant pleasure to us, to think that there is a God ; that he is such an one as the Scripture hath revealed him to be, a Being infinitely wise and powerful, holy, just, and good ; that this God governs the world, and gives law to all the creatures ; that he is our owner and ruler ; that in his hand our breath is, in his hand our times, our hearts, and all our ways, are.

Thus certainly it is, and thus it must be ; and happy they who can please themselves with these thoughts ! They must needs be a constant terror to themselves, who could wish it were otherwise.

They who thus delight in God have always something, and something very commanding too, to delight in ; a fountain of joy which can never be either exhausted or stopped up, and to which they may always have access. How few are there that " live many days," and " rejoice in them all !" Such a thing is supposed indeed, but it is never found true in any, except in those that make God their joy, the gladness of their joy; as the Psalmist expresses it, their " exceeding joy :" and in him it is intended the joy should terminate, when we are bid to " rejoice evermore," 1 Thess. v. 16.

VII. To be religious is to make a business of praising God. And is not this pleasant? It is indeed very unpleasant, and contrary to our inclination, to be obliged continually to praise one that is not worthy of praise; but what can be more pleasant than to praise him to whom all praise is due, and ours particularly; to whom we and all the creatures lie under all possible obligations; who is worthy of, and yet exalted far above, all blessing and praise; from whom all things are, and therefore to whom all things ought to be ?

There is little pleasure in praising one whom none praise that are wise and good, only the fools in Israel; but in praising God we concur with the blessed angels in heaven, and all the saints; and do it

in concert with them, who the more
they know him, the more they praise
him. " Bless the Lord, ye his angels,
and all his hosts ;" and therefore with
what pleasure can I cast my mite into
such a treasury ; " Bless the Lord, O
my soul !"

There is little pleasure in praising one,
who will not regard our praises, nor
take notice of our expressions of esteem
and affection ; but when we " offer to
God the sacrifice of praise continually,"
that is, " the fruit of our lips, giving
thanks to his name," we offer it to one
that takes notice of it, accepts it, is well
pleased with it, smells " a savour of rest"
from it, and will not fail to meet those
with his mercies, who follow him with
their praises ; for he has said, that they
who " offer praise glorify him ;" such
a favourable construction does he put
upon it, such a high stamp upon coarse
metal.

Now what is it that we have to do in
religion but to praise God? We are taken into a covenant with God, that we
should be to him " for a name, and for

a praise;" are called into his "marvellous light," that we should " shew forth the praises of him that called us." And how can we be more comfortably employed ? They are therefore " blessed that dwell in God's house, for they will be still praising him." And " it is a good thing," good in itself, and good for us, it is very pleasant, " to give thanks unto the Lord," and to " shew forth his praises;" for we cannot do ourselves a greater honour, or fetch in a greater satisfaction, than by " giving unto the Lord the glory due unto his name." It is not only a heaven upon earth, but it is a pledge and earnest of a heaven in heaven too; for if we be here " every day blessing God," we shall be " praising him for ever and ever;" for thus all who will go to heaven hereafter, begin their heaven now. Compare the hellish pleasure which some take in profaning the name of God, and the heavenly pleasure which others take in glorifying it, and tell me which is preferable.

VIII To be religious is to have all our inordinate appetites corrected, and regulated. And is not this also pleasant ? To be eased from pain is a sensible pleasure, and to be eased from that which is the disease and disorder of the mind, is a mental pleasure. Those certainly live a most unpleasant, uncomfortable life, who are slaves to their appetites, and indulge themselves in the gratifications of sense, though ever so criminal ; who lay the reins on the neck of their lusts, and withhold not their hearts from any joy. Drunkards and unclean persons, though they are said to give themselves up to their pleasures, yet really estrange themselves from that which is true pleasure, and subject themselves to a continual pain and uneasiness.

The carnal appetite is often overcharged, and that is a burden to the body, and its distemper. When enough is as good as a feast, I wonder what pleasure it can be to take more than enough ; and the appetite, the more it is indulged, the more humoursome and troublesome it grows ; it is surfeited and not satisfied ; it does but grow more impetuous, and more imperious. What Solomon says of a servant, is true of the body : " He that delicately bringeth up his servant from a child shall have him become his son," nay his master, " at the length." If we suffer the body to get dominion over the soul, so that the interests of the soul must be damaged to gratify the in-- clinations of the body, it will be a tyrant, as an usurper generally is, and will rule with rigour ; and as God said to the people, when by Samuel he had showed them " the manner of the king" that they chose, " You will cry out in that day because of your king which ye have chosen you, and the Lord will not hear ;" so it is with those that bring themselves into disorders, diseases, and terrors, by the indulgence of their lusts. Who can pity them ? They are well enough served for setting such a king over them. " Who hath woe ? Who hath sorrow ?" None so much as they that " tarry long at the wine," though they think themselves to have the mo-- nopoly of pleasure. The truth is, they who live in these pleasures are dead while they live," and while they fancy themselves to have the greatest liberty, really find themselves in the greatest slavery ; for they are " led captive by Satan at his will," and " of whom a man is overcome, of the same is he brought in bondage." And if the carnal appetite has not gained such a complete possession, as quite to extinguish all the remains of reason and conscience, those noble powers, since they are not permitted to give law, will give disturbance ; and there are few who have so full an enjoyment of the forbidden pleasures of sense, but that they sometimes feel the checks of reason and the terrors of conscience, which mar their mirth as the hand-writing on the wall did Belshazzar's, and make their lives uncomfortable to them, and justly so.

Now to be religious, is to have the exorbitant power of these lusts and appetites broken ; and since they will not be satisfied, to have them mortified and brought into a quiet submission to the commanding faculties of the soul, according to the direction of the divine law ; and thus peace is preserved, by support-

ing good order and government in the
soul. They certainly live the most easy,
healthful, pleasant lives, who are most
sober, temperate, and chaste ; who allow
not themselves to eat of any forbidden
tree, though " pleasant to the eye ;" who
live regularly, and are the masters, not
the servants, of " their own bellies ;" who
" keep under their bodies, and bring
them into subjection" to religion and
right reason ; and by laying the axe to
the root, and breaking through vicious
habits, dispositions, and desires, in the
strength of divine grace, have made the
refraining from vicious acts very easy
and pleasant. " If through the Spirit
we mortify the deeds of the body," we
live ; we live pleasantly.

IX. To be religious, is to have all our
unruly passions likewise governed and
subdued. And is not that pleasant?
Much of our torment arises from our in-
temperate hearts, discontent at the providence of God, fretfulness at every
cross occurrence, fear of every imaginary evil, envy at those who are in a
better state than ourselves, malice

against those who have injured us, and
an angry resentment of every, even the
least provocation. These are thorns and
briars in the soul. These spoil all enjoyment both of ourselves and of our friends,
and of our God too. These make men's
lives unpleasant, and make them a terror
to themselves and to all about them. But
when by the grace of God these " roots
of bitterness" are plucked up, which
bear so much " gall and wormwood,"
and we have learned of our Master to
be " meek and lowly in heart," we find
" rest to our souls," we enter into the
" pleasant land." There is scarcely any
of the graces of a Christian, that have
more of a present tranquillity and satisfaction, both inherent in them and an-
nexed to them, than this of meekness.
" The meek shall eat and be satisfied ;"
they shall " inherit the earth ;" they
shall " delight themselves in the abundance of peace ;" they shall " increase
their joy in the Lord," which nothing
diminishes more than ungoverned passion ; for that grieves the Spirit of grace,

the Comforter, and provokes him to withdraw.

X. To be religious is to dwell in love towards all our brethren, and to do all the good we can in this world. And is not that pleasant? Love is the " fulfilling of the law ;" it is the second great commandment, to "love our neighbour as ourselves." All our duty is summed up in one word, which, as it is a short word, so it is a sweet word—love. Behold how good and how pleasant it is to live in holy love ! It is not only pleasing to God, and amiable in the eyes of all good men, but it will be very comfortable to ourselves; for they that "dwell in love dwell in God, and God in them."

Religion teaches us to be kind to our relations, and to please them well in all things ; neither to give, nor resent provocations ; to bear with their infirmities ; to be courteous and obliging to all with whom we converse ; to keep our temper, and the possession and enjoyment of our own souls, whatever affronts are given

E

us. And can any thing contribute more
to our living pleasantly ?

By love we enjoy our friends, and
have communion with them in all their
comforts, and so add to our own; "rejoicing with them that do rejoice." By
love we recommend ourselves to their
love; and what more delightful than to
love and be beloved ? Love is the very
element of a pure and sanctified mind,
the sweet air it breathes in, the cement
of that society which contributes so
much to the pleasure of human life.
The sheep of Christ, united in flocks by
the bond of holy love, lie down together
in the "green pastures" by the "still
waters," where there is not only plenty,
but pleasure. The Apostle, exhorting
his friends to "be of good comfort," and
to go on cheerfully in their Christian
course, exhorts them, in order to that,
to "be of one mind, and to live in peace,"
and then, he says, "the God of love and
peace will be with them."

And what pleasure is comparable to
that of doing good ? It is some parti-
cipation of the pleasure of the Eternal

Mind, who delights to show mercy, and to do good. Nay, besides the divinity of this pleasure, there is a humanity in it. The nature of man, if he be not debauched and vitiated, cannot but take pleasure in making any-body safe and easy. It was a pleasure to Job, to think that he had " caused the widow's heart to sing for joy," had been " eyes to the blind, feet to the lame, and a father to the poor," and that they had been " warmed with the fleece of his sheep." The pleasure that a good man has in doing good, confirms that saying of our Saviour's, that " it is more blessed to give than to receive."

XI. To be religious is to live a life of communion with God. And is not this pleasant ? Good Christians, being taken into friendship, have " fellowship with the Father, and with his Son Jesus Christ," (1 John i. 3.) and make it their business to keep up that holy converse and correspondence. Herein consists the life of religion, to converse with God, to receive his communications of mercy and grace to us, and to return pious and

devout affections to him; and can any
life be more comfortable? Is there any
conversation that can possibly be so pleasant as this, to a soul that knows itself,
and its own powers and interests?

In reading and meditating upon the
word of God, we hear God speaking
with a great deal of condescension to us
and concern for us, speaking freely to us
as a man does to his friend, and about
our own business; speaking comfortably
to us in compassion to our distressful
case; and what can be more pleasant to
those who have a value for the favour
of God, and care about the interests of
their own souls? "When their judges
are overthrown in stony places, they
shall hear my words, for they are sweet:"
the words of God will be very sweet to
those who see themselves overthrown
by sin; and so they will be to all that
love God. With what an air of pleasure does the spouse say, "It is the
voice of my beloved, and he speaks to
me!"—In prayer and praise we speak to
God, and we have liberty of speech,
have leave to "utter all our words be-

fore the Lord," as Jephtha did his in
Mizpeh, Judges xi. 11. We speak to
one whose ear is open, is bowed down to
our prayers, nay, to whom the "prayer
of the upright" is a "delight." It is not
only an ease to a burdened spirit to unbosom itself to such a friend as God is,
but a pleasure to a soul that knows its
own extraction, to have such a "boldness" as all believers have, to "enter into the holiest."—We may as truly have
communion with God in providences, as
in ordinances; and in the duties of common conversation, as in religious exercises; and thus that pleasure may become
a continual feast to our souls. What can
be more pleasant than to have a God to
go to, whom we may "acknowledge in
all our ways," and whom our "eyes are
ever towards?" to see all our comforts
coming to us from his hand, and all our
crosses too? to refer ourselves, and all
events that concern us, to his disposal,
with an assurance that he will order all
for the best? What a pleasure it is to
behold the beauty of the Lord in all his
works, and to taste the goodness of the

Lord in all his gifts; in all our expectations to see every man's judgment proceeding from him; to make God our hope, and God our fear, and God our joy, and God our life, and God our all! This is to live a life of communion with God.

XII. To be religious is to keep up a constant expectation of "the glory to be revealed." It is to set eternal life before us as the mark we aim at, and the prize we run for, and to seek the things that are above. And is not this pleasant? It is our duty to think much of heaven, to place our happiness in its joys, and thitherward to direct our aims and pursuits; and what subject, what object can be more pleasing? We have need sometimes to frighten ourselves from sin with the terrors of eternal death; but it is much more a part of our religion, to encourage ourselves in our duty with the hopes of that eternal life which God hath given us, that "life which is in his Son."

What is Christianity, but "having our conversation in heaven," trading with the New Jerusalem, and keeping up a constant correspondence with that better country, that is the heavenly, as the country we belong to, and are in expectation of; to which we remit our best effects and best affections; where our head and home is, and where we hope and long to be?

Then we are as we should be, when our minds are in a heavenly frame and temper; then we do as we should do, when we are employed in the heavenly work, as we are capable of doing it in this lower world; and is not our religion then a heaven upon earth? If there be a fulness of joy and pleasure in that glory and happiness, which is grace and holiness perfected, there cannot but be an abundance of joy and pleasure in that grace and holiness, which is glory and happiness begun. If there will be such a complete satisfaction in vision and fruition, there cannot but be a great deal in faith and hope so well founded as that of the saints is. Hence we are said, when believing, to "rejoice with joy unspeakable," and to be "filled with joy and peace in believing."

It is the character of all God's people, that they are born from heaven, and bound for heaven, and have laid up their treasure in heaven ; and they who know how great, how rich, how glorious, and how well secured that happiness is to all believers, cannot but own, that if that be their character, it cannot but be their unspeakable comfort and delight.

Now sum up the whole, and then tell me whether religion be not a pleasant thing indeed, when even the duties of it are so much the delights of it; and whether we do not serve a good Master, who has thus made our work its own wages, and has graciously provided two heavens for those that never deserved one

CHAPTER III

THE PLEASANTNESS OF RELIGION PROVED
FROM THE PROVISION THAT IS MADE
FOR THE COMFORT OF THOSE WHO ARE
RELIGIOUS, AND THE PRIVILEGES THEY
ARE ENTITLED TO.

WE have already found by inquiry,
(oh that we could all say we had found
by experience!) that the very principles
and practices of religion have a great
deal of pleasantness in them, and the
one half of it has not been told us; and
yet the comfort that attends religion
and follows after it, cannot but exceed
that which is inherent in it, and comes
with it. If the " work of righteousness
be peace," much more is the " effect of

righteousness" so. If the precepts of religion have such an air of sweetness in them, what then have the comforts of it? Behold, " happy is the people," even in this world, " whose God is the Lord."

We must conclude, that they who walk in the ways of holy Wisdom, have, or may have, true peace and pleasure ; for God has both taken care for their comfort, and given them cause to be comforted ; so that if they do not live easily and pleasantly, it is their own fault.

I. The God whom they serve, has taken care for their comfort, and has done enough to convince them, that it is his will they should be comforted ; that he not only gives them leave to be cheerful, but would have them to be so ; for what could have been done more to the satisfaction of his family, than he has done in it ?

1. There is a purchase made of peace and pleasure for them, so that they come to it fairly, and by a good title. He that purchased them a peculiar people to himself, took care that they should

be a pleasant people, that their comforts might be a credit to his cause, and the joy of his servants in this work might be a reputation to his family. We have not only " peace with God through our Lord Jesus Christ," but peace in our own consciences too ; not only peace above but peace within ; and nothing less will pacify an offended conscience, than that which satisfied an offended God. Yet this is not all ; we have not only inward peace, but we " rejoice in the hope of the glory of God," and triumph over, nay, we triumph " in tribulation."

Think what a vast expense, if I may so say, God was at of blood and treasure, to lay up for us, and to secure to us, not only a future bliss, but present pleasure, and the felicities not only of our home, but of our way. Christ had trouble, that we might have peace— pain, that we might have pleasure— sorrow, that we might have joy. He wore the crown of thorns, that he might crown us with roses, and a lasting joy might be upon our heads. He put on

the " spirit of heaviness," that we might
be arrayed with the "garments of praise."
The garden was the place of his agony,
that it might be to us a garden of Eden ;
and there it'was that he covenanted with
his prosecutors for his disciples, upon
his surrendering himself, saying in effect
to all agonies, as he did to them, " If
ye seek me, let these go their way;" if
I be resigned to trouble, let them "depart in peace."

This was that which made Wisdom's
ways pleasantness—" the everlasting
righteousness" which Christ, by dying,
wrought out and brought in. This is
the foundation of the treaty of peace,
and consequently the fountain of all
those consolations which believers are
happy in. Then it is, that " all the
seed of Israel glory," when they can
each of them say, " In the Lord have
I righteousness and strength ;" and then
Israel shall dwell safely, in a holy security, where they have learned to call
Christ by this name, " the Lord our
Righteousness." If Christ had not gone
to the Father as our High Priest, with

"the blood of sprinkling" in his hand, we could never have rejoiced, but must have been always trembling.

Christ is our peace, not only as he made peace for us with God, but as he "preached" to them "that were far off and to them that were nigh," and has engaged that his people, whenever they may have trouble in the world, shall have "peace in him;" upon the assurance of which, they may be of good cheer, whatever happens. It is observable, that in the close of that ordinance which Christ instituted in the night wherein he was betrayed, to be a memorial of his sufferings, he both sung a hymn of joy and preached a sermon of comfort, to intimate, that what he designed in dying for us, was to give us "everlasting consolation and good hope through grace;" and this we should aim at in all our commemorations of his death.

Peace and comfort are bought and paid for; if any of those who were designed to have the benefit of this purchase, deprive themselves of it, let them

bear the blame, but let him have the
praise who intended them the kindness,
and who will take care that though his
kindness be deferred, it shall not be
defeated; for though his disciples may
be sorrowful for a time, "their sorrow
shall be turned into joy."

2. There are "promises made" to believers, of peace and pleasure. The
benefits Christ bought for them are
conveyed to them, and settled upon
them in the covenant of grace; which
is "well ordered in all things," for the
comfort and satisfaction of those, who
have made that covenant "all their
salvation and all their desire."

There it is that "light is sown for
the righteous," and it will come up in
due time. The promises of that covenant are the "wells of salvation," out
of which they "draw water with joy;"
the "breasts of consolation," out of which
by faith they are satisfied.

Those promises of the Old Testament,
which point at the gospel times, speak
mostly of this as the blessing reserved
for those times, that there should be

great joy and rejoicing. The design of the gospel was to make religion a more pleasant thing than it had been, by freeing it both from the burdensome services which the Jews were under, and from the superstitious fears with which the heathens kept themselves in awe ; and by enlarging the privileges of God's people, and making them easier to come at.

Every particular believer is interested in the promises made to the church, and may plead them, and fetch in the comfort contained in them ; as every citizen has the benefit of a charter, even the meanest. What a pleasure may one take in applying such a promise as this, " I will never leave thee nor forsake thee ?" or this, " All things shall work together for good to them that love God ?" These, and such as these, " guide our feet into the ways of peace." And as they are a firm foundation on which to build our hopes, so they are a full fountain from which to draw our joys. By the exceeding great and precious promises, we partake of a divine nature in this instance of it, as much as in any—

a comfortable enjoyment of ourselves, and by all the other promises, that promise is fulfilled—" My servants shall eat, but ye shall be hungry; my servants shall drink, but ye shall be thirsty; my servants shall rejoice, but ye shall be ashamed; my servants shall sing for joy of heart, but ye shall cry for sorrow of heart; and the encouragement given to all the church's faithful friends, is made good, " rejoice ye with Jerusalem, and be glad with her all ye that love her."

3. There is provision made for the application of that which is purchased and promised to the saints. What will it avail that there is wine in the vessel, if it be not drawn out? that there is a cordial made up, if it be not administered? Care is therefore taken, that the people of God be assisted in making use of the comforts treasured up for them in the everlasting covenant.

A religious life, one may well expect, should be a very comfortable life; for infinite wisdom has devised all the means that could be devised to make it so. What could have been done more for

God's vineyard, to make it flourishing as well as fruitful, than what he has done in it? There is not only an overflowing fulness of oil in the good olive, but "golden pipes," for the conveyance of that oil to the lamps, to keep them burning, Zech. iv. 12. When God would himself furnish a paradise for a beloved creature, there was nothing wanting that might contribute to the comfort of it; in it was planted "every tree that was pleasant to the sight, and good for food;" so in the gospel there is a paradise planted for all the faithful offspring of the second Adam : a Canaan, a land "flowing with milk and honey, a pleasant land, a rest" for all the spiritual seed of Abraham. Now, as God put Adam into Paradise, and brought Israel into Canaan, so he has provided for giving possession to all believers of all that comfort and pleasure which is laid up for them. As in the garden of Eden innocency and pleasure were twined together, so in the gospel of Christ, grace and peace, "righteousness and peace have kissed each other;" and all is done that could be

D

wished, in order to our "entering into this rest," this blessed Sabbath. So that if we have not the benefit of it, we may thank ourselves. God would have comforted us, and we would not be comforted; our souls refused it.

Four things are done with this view, that those who live a godly life may live a comfortable and pleasant life; and it is a pity that they should receive the grace of God herein in vain.

First: the blessed Spirit is sent to be the Comforter. He enlightens, convinces, and sanctifies, but he has his name from this part of his office; he is "the Comforter." As the "Son of God" was sent to be the "Consolation of Israel," to provide matter for comfort, so the Spirit of God was sent to be "the Comforter," to apply the consolation which the Lord Jesus had provided. Christ came to make peace, and the Spirit to seek peace, and to "make us hear joy and gladness," even such as will cause broken bones themselves to rejoice. Christ having wrought out salvation for us, the work of the Spirit is to give us the comfort of it. Hence the joy of the saints is said to be "the joy of the Holy Ghost," because it is his office to administer such comforts as tend to fill us with joy.

The Spirit, as a Comforter, was given not only for the relief of the saints in the suffering ages of the church, but to continue " with the church alway to the end," for the comfort of believers, in reference to their constant sorrows, both temporal and spiritual; and what a favour is this to the church! no less needful, no less advantageous, than the sending of the Son of God to save us; and for this therefore we should be no less thankful. Let this article never be left out of our songs of praise, but let us always give thanks to him, who not only sent his Son to make satisfaction for us, but sent his Spirit to give satisfaction to us; sent his Spirit not only to work in us the disposition of children towards him, but also to witness to our adoption, and " seal us to the day of redemption."

The Spirit is given to be our teacher,

and to " lead us into all truth," and as
such he is a Comforter ; for by rectify-
ing our mistakes, and setting things in
a true light, he silences our doubts and
fears, and sets things in a pleasant light.
The Spirit is our Remembrancer, to put
us in mind of that which we know, and
as such he is a Comforter ; for, like the
disciples, we distrust Christ in every
exigence, because we " forget the mi-
racles of the loaves."—The Spirit is our
Sanctifier ; by him sin is mortified, and
grace wrought and strengthened ; and
as such he is our Comforter ; for nothing
tends so much to make us easy, as that
which tends to make us holy.—The
Spirit is our Guide ; we are said to be
" led by the Spirit ;" and as such he is
our Comforter ; for under his conduct
we cannot but be led into " ways of
pleasantness," to the " green pastures,"
and " still waters."

Secondly : the Scriptures are written,
" that our joy may be full ;" that we
may have that joy which alone is filling,
and has that in it which will fill up the
vacancies of other joys, and make up

their deficiences, and that we may be full of that joy, may have more and more of it, may be wholly taken up with it, and may come at length to the full perfection of it in the kingdom of glory. "These things are written to you," not only that you may "receive the word with joy" at first, when it is a new thing to you, but that your "joy may be full" and constant. The word of God is the chief conveyance by which comfort is communicated from Christ, the fountain of life, to all the saints.

The scriptures we may have always with us, and whenever we will, we may have recourse to them ; so that we need not have to seek for cordials at any time. The " word is nigh thee," in thy house, and in thy hand, and it is thine own fault if it be not in thy mouth and in thy heart. Nor is it a spring shut up, or "a fountain sealed." Those that compare spiritual things with spiritual, will find the scripture its own interpreter ; and spiritual pleasure to flow from it as easily, as plentifully, to all

who have spiritual senses exercised, as
the honey from the comb.

The saints have found pleasure in the
word of God, and all those who have
given up themselves to be led and ruled
by it. It was such a comfort to David
in his distress, that if he had not had
that for his delight, he would have pe-
rished in his affliction ; nay, he had the
joy of God's word to be his continual
entertainment :   "Thy statutes have
been my songs in the house of my pil-
grimage."—"Thy words were found,"
says Jeremiah, "and I did eat them,"
feast upon them with as much pleasure
as ever any hungry man did upon his
necessary food, or epicure upon his
dainties : I perfectly regaled myself with
them ; and " thy word was unto me the
joy and rejoicing of my heart."   And we
not only come short of their experience,
but frustrate God's gracious intentions, if
we do not find pleasure in the word of
God ; for " whatsoever things were written aforetime, were written for our learning ; that we, through patience and comfort of the Scriptures, might have hope "

Thirdly: holy ordinances were instituted for the furtherance of our comfort, and to make our religion pleasant unto us. The conversation of friends with each other, is reckoned one of the greatest delights of this world: now ordinances are instituted for the keeping up of our communion with God, which is the greatest delight of the soul that is allied to the other world. God appointed to the Jewish church a great many feasts in the year, and but one fast, and that but for one day, for this end, that they might "rejoice before the Lord their God," they and their families, Deut. xvi. 11.

Prayer is an ordinance of God, appointed for the fetching in of that peace and pleasure which are provided for us. It is intended to be not only the ease of our hearts by casting our burden upon God, as it was to Hannah, who, when she had prayed, "went her way, and did eat, and her countenance was no more sad;" but to be the joy of our hearts, by putting the promises in suit, and improving our acquaintance with heaven: "Ask, and ye shall receive, that your joy may be full." There is a throne of grace erected for us to come to: a Mediator of grace appointed, in whose name to come; the Spirit of grace given to help our infirmities; and an answer of peace promised to every prayer of faith: and all this, that we may fetch in, not only sanctifying, but comforting grace "in every time of need." God's house, in which Wisdom's children dwell, is called "a house of prayer," and thither God brings them, on purpose to "make them joyful."

Singing of psalms is a gospel ordinance that is designed to contribute to the pleasantness of our religion; not only to express, but to excite and to increase our holy joy. In singing to the Lord, we make a "joyful noise to the rock of our salvation." When the apostle had warned all Christians to take heed of drunkenness, "Be not drunk with wine, wherein is excess," lest they should think that thereby he restrained them from any mirth that would do them good, he directs them, instead of the song of the drunkard, when the heart is merry, to entertain themselves with the songs of angels: "Speaking to yourselves in psalms and hymns, and spiritual songs; singing and making melody in your hearts to the Lord." There is no substance in this ordinance, but God, in condescension to our state, has been pleased to make a particular ordinance of it, to show how much it is his will that we should be cheerful. "Is any merry? let him sing psalms." Is any vainly merry? let him suppress the vanity, and turn the mirth into a right channel. He need not banish nor abjure the mirth, but let it be holy, heavenly mirth, and in that mirth, "let him sing psalms." Nay, "is any afflicted," and merry in his affliction? let him show it by singing psalms, as Paul and Silas did "in the stocks."—The Lord's day is appointed to be a pleasant day, a day of holy rest, nay, and a day too of holy joy; a thanksgiving day: "This is the day which the Lord hath made, we will rejoice and be glad in it."—The Lord's Supper is a spiritual feast; and a feast, Solomon says, "was made for laughter," and so was this for holy joy. We celebrate the memorials of his death, that we may rejoice in the victories he obtained, and the purchases he made by his death; and may apply to ourselves the privileges and comforts, which by the covenant of grace are made our's. There we cannot but be glad, and "rejoice in him, where we remember his love more than wine."

Fourthly: the ministry is appointed for the comfort of the saints, and their guides in the ways of wisdom are instructed by all means possible, to make them "ways of pleasantness," and to encourage them to go on pleasantly in those ways. The priests of old were "ordained for men," and were therefore "taken from among men," that they might have compassion upon the mourners. And the prophets had this particularity in their commission, "Comfort ye, comfort ye, my people, saith your God; speak ye comfortably to Jerusalem."

Thus has God taken care for the comfort of his people, so that he is not to be blamed if they be not comforted. But this is not all.

II. There are many particular benefits and privileges which they are entitled to, who walk in the ways of religion, that contribute very much to the pleasantness of those ways. By the blood of Christ those benefits and privileges are procured for them, which speaks them highly valuable; and by the covenant of grace they are secured to them, which speaks them unalienable.

1. Those who walk in Wisdom's ways are discharged from the debts of sin, and that is pleasant. They are privileged from arrests. "Who shall lay any thing to their charge," while "it is God that justifies" them, and will stand by his own act, against hell and earth? and he is always near that justifies them; and so is their Advocate, who pleads for them, nearer than their accuser, though he stand at their right hand to resist them; and he is able to cast him out, and all his accusations.

Surely they put a force upon themselves who are merry and pleasant under the guilt of sin; for if conscience be awake, it cannot but have "a fearful looking for of vengeance;" but if sin be done away, the burden is removed, the wound is healed, and all is well. "Son, be of good cheer," said Christ; though sick of a palsy, yet be cheerful; for "thy sins are forgiven thee;" and therefore, not only they shall not hurt thee, but God is reconciled to thee, and will do thee good; thou mayest enjoy the comforts of this life, and fear no snare in them; mayest bear the crosses of this life, and feel no sting in them; and mayest look forward to another life without terror or amazement.

The pain which true penitents experience in reflecting upon their sins, make the pleasure and satisfaction they have in the assurance of the pardon of them doubly sweet; as the sorrow of a woman in travail is not an allay but rather an increase to the joy, that a "man is born into the world:" no pain is more acute than that of broken bones, to

which the sorrows of a penitent sinner
are compared; but when they are well
set and well knit again, they are not
only made easy, but they are made to
rejoice; and to this the comforts of a
pardoned sinner are compared. " Make
me to hear joy and gladness, that the
bones which thou hast broken may rejoice," Psalm li. 8. All our bones,
when kept that not one of them was
broken, must say, " Lord, who is like
unto thee?" but there is a more sensible
joy for one displaced bone reduced, than
for the multitude of the bones that
were never hurt; for one lost sheep
brought home, than for ninety and nine
that went not astray. Such is the pleasure which they have, who know their
sins are pardoned.

When God's prophets must speak
comfortably to Jerusalem, they must
tell her that " her iniquity is pardoned."
Such a pleasure there is in the sense of
the forgiveness of sins, that it enables
us to make a light matter of temporal
afflictions, particularly that of sickness;
" the inhabitants shall not say, I am

sick, for the people that dwell therein shall be forgiven their iniquity;"—and to make a great matter of temporal mercies, when they are thus sweetened and secured, particularly that of recovery from sickness; " Thou hast, in love to my soul," cured my body, and " delivered it from the pit of corruption, for thou hast cast all my sins behind thy back." If our sins be pardoned, and we know it, we may go out and come in in peace, nothing can come amiss to us; we may lie down and rise up with pleasure; for all is clear between us and heaven; thus "blessed is the man whose iniquity is forgiven."

2. They have "the Spirit of God witnessing with their spirits, that they are the children of God," and that is pleasant. Can the children of princes and great men please themselves with the thoughts of the honours and expectations which attend that relationship? And may not the children of God think with pleasure on the adoption they have received? And the pleasure must be the greater, and make the stronger im-

pressions of joy, when they remember, that they were by nature not only strangers and foreigners, but children of wrath, and yet are thus highly favoured. The comfort of relations is none of the least of the delights of this life, but what comfort of relations is comparable to this of being related to God as our Father, and to Christ as our elder brother; and to all the saints and angels too, as belonging to the same family, which we are happily brought into relation to? The pleasure of claiming and owning this relation is plainly intimated in our being taught to cry, " Abba, Father ;" why should it be thus doubled, and in two languages, but to intimate to us, the unaccountable pleasure and satisfaction, with which good Christians call God " Father?" It is the string they harp upon, " Abba, Father."

3. They have " access with boldness to the throne of grace ;" and that is pleasant. Prayer not only fetches in peace and pleasure, but it is itself a great privilege, and not only an honour but a comfort. It is one of the greatest

comforts of our lives, that we have a God to go to at all times, so that we need not fear coming unseasonably or coming too often ; and in all places we may go to him, though we are as Jonah in the fish's belly, or as David in the " depths," or " in the ends of the earth."

It is a pleasure to one who is full of care and grief, to unbosom himself ; and to one who wants or fears wanting, to petition one that is able and willing to supply his wants. And we have great encouragement to "make our requests known to God ;" we have " access with confidence," not access with difficulty, as we have to great men, nor access with uncertainty of acceptance, as the Ninevites, " Who can tell if God will return to us ?" but we have access with assurance. " Whatsoever we ask" in faith, according to his will, " we know that we have the petitions that we desired of him."

It is a pleasure to talk to one whom we love, and who, we know, loves us, and though far above us, yet takes notice of what we say, and is tenderly concerned for us; what a pleasure is it then to speak to God! to have not only a liberty of access, but a liberty of speech, freedom to utter all our mind, humbly and in faith; "boldness to enter into the holiest by the blood of Jesus;" and boldness to pour out our hearts before God, as one who, though he knows our case better than we ourselves, yet will give us the satisfaction of knowing it from us, according to our own showing. Beggars who have good benefactors, live as pleasantly as any other people; this is the case of God's people, they are beggars, but they are beggars to a bountiful Benefactor, that is "rich in mercy to all that call upon him:" blessed are they that "wait daily at the posts of wisdom's doors." If the prayer of the upright be God's delight, it cannot but be their's.

4. They have a sanctified use of all their creature comforts, and that is pleasant. What God's people have, be it little or much, they have it from the love of God, and with his blessing; and then behold, all things are clean and sweet

to them ; they come from the hand of
a Father, by the hand of a Mediator, not
in the channel of common providence,
but by the golden pipes of the promises
of the covenant. And hence it is, that
"a little that a righteous man hath,"
having a heart to be content with it, and
the divine skill of enjoying God in it, is
better to him than the riches of many
wicked are to them ; and that "a dinner
of herbs, where love is," and the "fear
of the Lord," is better, and yields abundantly more satisfaction, than "a stalled
ox, and hatred and trouble therewith."

5. They have the testimony of their
own consciences for them in all condi-
tions ; and that is pleasant. A good conscience is not only a brazen wall, but a
continual feast ; and all the melody of
Solomon's instruments of music of all
sorts, were not to be compared with that
of the bird in the bosom when it sings
sweet. If Paul has a "conscience void
of offence," though he be "as sorrowful,
yet he is always rejoicing ;" nay, and
even when he is "pressed above measure," and has "received a sentence of

death within himself," his rejoicing is this, even the testimony of his conscience concerning his integrity.

As nothing is more painful and unpleasant than to be smitten and reproached by our own hearts, to have our consciences fly in our faces, and give us our own; so there is nothing more comfortable, than to be upon good grounds reconciled to ourselves; to prove our own work by the touchstone of God's word, and to find it right, for then have we rejoicing in ourselves alone, and not in another; for "if our hearts condemn us not, then have we confidence towards God;" may lift up our face without spot unto him, and comfortably appeal to his omniscience; "Thou, O Lord, knowest me; thou hast seen me, and tried my heart towards thee." It is easy to imagine the holy humble pleasure that a good man has in the just reflection upon the successful resistance of a strong and threatening temptation; the seasonable suppressing and crossing of an unruly appetite or passion, and a check given to the

tongue when it was about to speak un-
advisedly. What a pleasure is it to look
back upon any good word spoken, or
any good work done, in the strength of
God's grace, to his glory, and any way
to the advantage of our brethren, either
for soul or body! With what a sweet
satisfaction may a good man lie down in
the close of the Lord's day, if God has
enabled him, in some measure, to do the
work of the day in the day, according
as the duty of the day requires! We
may then eat our bread with joy, and
drink our wine with a merry heart,
when we have some good ground to hope
that God now accepteth our works
through Jesus Christ.

6. They have the earnests and foretastes of eternal life and glory; and that
is pleasant indeed. They have it not
only secured to them, but dwelling in
them, in the first fruits of it, such as they
are capable of in their present imperfect
state; "These things are written unto
you that believe on the name of the Son
of God, that ye may know," not only
that you shall have, but "that you have

eternal life;" you are " sealed with that
Holy Spirit of promise," which is the
" earnest of our inheritance," not only a
ratification of the grant, but part of the
full payment.

Canaan, when we come to it, will be
a land flowing with milk and honey;
" in God's presence there is fulness of
joy, and pleasures for evermore;" but
lest we should think it long ere we come
to it, the God whom we serve has been
pleased to send to us, as he did to Israel,
some clusters of the grapes of that good
land, to meet us in the wilderness. Now
if they were sent us in excuse of the full
enjoyment, and we were to be put off
with them, that would put a bitterness
into them; but being sent us in earnest
of the full enjoyment, that puts a sweetness into them, and makes them pleasant indeed.

A day in God's courts, and an hour at
his table in communion with him, is very
pleasant, better than a thousand days,
than ten thousand hours, in any of the
enjoyments of sense; but this very much
increases the pleasantness of it, that it is

the pledge of a blessed eternity, which we hope to spend "within the veil," in the vision and fruition of God. Sabbaths are sweet, as they are the earnests of the everlasting sabbatism, or keeping of a sabbath, as the apostle calls it, Heb. iv. 9, which "remaineth for the people of God." Gospel feasts are therefore sweet, because earnests of the everlasting feast to which we shall sit down with Abraham, and Isaac, and Jacob. The joys of the Holy Ghost are sweet, as they are earnests of that joy of our Lord, into which all Christ's good and faithful servants shall enter. Praising God is sweet, as it is an earnest of that blessed state in which we shall not rest day or night from praising God. The communion of saints is sweet, as it is an earnest of the pleasure we hope to have in the "general assembly and church of the first-born."

They that travel in Wisdom's ways, though sometimes they find themselves walking in the low and darksome "valley of the shadow of death," where they can see but a little way before them;

yet at other times are led with Moses to the top of Mount Pisgah, and thence have a pleasant prospect of the land of promise, and the glories of that good land; not with such a damp upon the pleasure of it as Moses had, "Thou shalt see it with thine eyes, but thou shalt not go over thither;" but such an addition to the pleasure of it as Abraham had, when God said to him, "All the land which thou seest, to thee will I give it." Take the pleasure of the prospect, as a pledge of the possession shortly.

CHAPTER IV.

THE DOCTRINE FURTHER PROVED BY EXPERIENCE.

HAVING found religion in its own nature pleasant, and the comforts and privileges so, with which it is attended ; we shall next try to make this truth more evident, by appealing to such as may be thought competent witnesses in such a case. I confess if we appeal to the "natural man," who looks no further than the things of sense, and judges by no other rule than sense, and "receiveth not the things of the Spirit of God," for they are "foolishness to him ;" such a one will be so far from consenting to this truth, and concurring with it, that he will contradict and oppose it. Our appeal must be to those who have some spiritual senses exercised, " for the brutish man knows not, neither doth the fool understand this." We must therefore be allowed to appeal to convinced sinners, and comforted saints. Wicked people, whom the Spirit has roused out of a sinful security, and godly people, whom the Spirit has put to rest in a holy serenity, are the most competent witnesses to give evidence in this case ; and to their experience we appeal.

I. Ask those who have tried the ways of sin and wickedness, of vice and profaneness, and begin to pause a little, and to consider, whether the way they are in be right ; and let us hear what is their experience concerning those ways : and our appeal to them is in the words of the apostle, "What fruit had ye then in those things, whereof ye are now ashamed ?" Not only what fruit will ye have at last, when the end of these things is death ; or, "What pleasure hath he in his house after him, when the number of his months is cut off in the midst ?" but what fruit, what pleasure had ye then, when you were in the enjoyment of the best of it?

Those who have been running to an excess of riot, who have laid the reins on the neck of their lusts, have rejoiced with the " young man in his youth, and walked in the way of their hearts and the sight of their eyes," have taken a boundless liberty in the gratification of sense, and have made it their business to extract out of this world whatever may pass under the name of pleasure: ask them now, when they begin to reflect, which they could not find in their hearts to do while they were going on in their pursuit—ask them what they think of those pleasures which pretend to vie with those of religion, and they will tell you,

1. That the pleasure of sin was painful and unsatisfying in the enjoyment, and a pleasure which then they had no reason to boast of. It was a sordid pleasure, and beneath the dignity of a man, and which could not be had, but by yielding up the throne in the soul to the inferior faculties of sense, and allowing

them the dominion over reason and conscience, which ought to command and give law. It was the gratifying of an appetite which was the disease of the soul, and which would not be satisfied, but, like the daughters of the horse-leech, still cried, " Give, give."

They who have made themselves slaves to their lusts, will own, that it was the greatest drudgery in the world, and therefore is represented in the parable of the prodigal by a young gentleman hiring himself to one that sent him into his field to feed swine, where he was made a fellow-commoner with them, and " would fain have filled his belly with the husks" that they did eat ; such a disgrace, such a dissatisfaction, is there in the pleasures of sin. And consider, too, the diversity of masters which sinners are at the beck of, and their disagreement among themselves ; for they that are disobedient to that God who is One, are deceived, " serving divers lusts and pleasures," and therein " led captive" by Satan, their sworn enemy, " at his will."

2. They will tell you that the pleasure of sin was very bitter, and tormenting in the reflection. We will allow that there is a pleasure in sin for a season, but that season is soon over, and is succeeded by another season that is the reverse of it ; the sweetness is soon gone, and leaves the bitterness behind in the bottom of the cup : the wine is red, and gives " its colour ;" its flavour is very agreeable, but at the last it " bites like a serpent, and stings like an adder." Sin is that strange woman, whose flatteries are charming, but " her end bitter as wormwood."

When conscience is awake, and tells the sinner he is verily guilty ; when his sins are set in order before him in their true colour, and he sees himself defiled and deformed by them ; when his own wickedness begins to correct him, and his backslidings to reprove him, and his own heart makes him " loathe himself for his abominations," where is the pleasure of his sin then ? As the thief is ashamed when he is discovered to the world, so are the drunkards, the unclean, when discovered to themselves. They say, " Where shall I cause my shame to go ?" There is no remedy, but I must " lie down in it." If the pleasure of any sin would last, surely that of ill-got gain would, because there is something to show for it; and yet, though that wickedness be sweet in the sinner's mouth, though he " hide it under his tongue, yet in his bowels it is turned into the gall of asps." He hath " swallowed down riches," but shall be forced to " vomit them up again."

And is such pleasure as this worthy to come in competition with the pleasures of religion, or to be named the same day with them ? What senseless creatures are the sensual, that will not be persuaded to quit the pleasures of brutes, when they might have in exchange the delights of angels !

II. Ask those that have tried the ways of wisdom, what is their experience concerning those ways. " Call now, if there be any that will answer you, and to which of the saints will you turn ?" Turn you to which you will, and they

will agree to this, that " Wisdom's ways
are pleasantness, and her paths peace."
However about some things they may
differ in their sentiments, in this they
are all of a mind, that God is a good
master, and his service not only perfect
freedom, but perfect pleasure. And it
is a debt which aged and experienced
Christians owe both to their Master and
to their fellow-servants, both to Christ
and to Christians, to bear their testimony
to this truth ; and the more explicitly
and solemnly they do it, the better.
Let them tell others " what God has
done for their souls," and how they have
" tasted that he is gracious ;" let them
own to the honour of God and religion,
that there " has not failed one word of
God's good promise ;" by which he designed to make his service pleasant;
that what is said of the pleasantness of
religion is really true. Let them " set
to their seal that' it is true."

The ways of religion and godliness
are the good old ways. Now, if you
would have an account of the way you
are to go, you must inquire of those

that have travelled it, not those who have only occasionally stept into it, but those whose business has led them to frequent it. Ask the ancient travellers whether they have found rest to their souls in this way, and there are few you shall inquire of, but will be ready to own these four things from experience—

1. That they have found the rules and dictates of religion very agreeable both to right reason, and to their true interest, and therefore pleasant. They have found all God's precepts concerning all things to be right and reasonable, and highly equitable; and when they did but show themselves men, they could not but consent and subscribe "to the law, that it is good." And there is a wonderful propriety in this; for the laws of humility and meekness, sobriety and temperance, contentment and patience, love and charity, are agreeable to ourselves, when we are in our right mind. They are the rectitude of our nature, the advancement of our powers and faculties, the composure of our minds, and

the comfort of our lives, and carry their own letters of commendation along with them. If a man understood himself and his own interest, he would comport with these rules, and govern himself by them, though there were no authority over him to oblige him to it. All that have thoroughly tried them, will say they are so far from being chains of imprisonment to a man, and as fetters to his feet, that they are as chains of ornament to him, and as the girdle to his loins. Ask experienced Christians, and they will tell you what abundance of comfort and satisfaction they have had in keeping sober, when they have been in temptation to excess ; in doing justly, when they might have gained by dishonesty, as others do, and nobody know it ; in forgiving an injury, when it was in the power of their hand to revenge it ; in giving alms to the poor, when perhaps they straitened themselves by it ; in submitting to an affliction, when the circumstances of it were very aggravating ; and in bridling their passion under great provocations. With what comfort

does Nehemiah reflect upon it, that
though his predecessors in the government had abused their power, yet " so
did not I, because of the fear of God !"
And with what pleasure does Samuel
make his appeal, "Whose ox have I
taken, or whom have I defrauded ?" and
Paul his; "I have coveted no man's
silver, or gold, or apparel !" If you
would have a register of experiences
to this purpose, read the 119th Psalm,
which is a collection of David's testimonies to the sweetness and goodness of God's
law, the equity and excellency of it, and
the abundant satisfaction that is to be
found in a constant conscientious con-
formity to it.

2. They will say also that they have
found the exercises of devotion to be
very pleasant and comfortable; and if
there be a heaven upon earth, it is in
communion with God in his ordinances;
in hearing from him, in speaking to him,
in receiving the tokens of his favour and
communications of his grace, and re-
turning pious affections to him : pour-
ing out the heart before him; lifting up

H

the soul to him. All good Christians
will subscribe to David's experience;
' It is good for me to draw near to God :"
the nearer the better ; and it will be best
of all when I come to the nearest of all
within the vail, and shall join with them
in saying, " Return unto thy rest, O my
soul !" to God as to thy rest, and repose
in him. I have found that satisfaction
in communion with God, which I would
not exchange for all the delights of the
sons of men, and the peculiar treasures
of kings and provinces.

What a pleasure did those pious Jews
in Hezekiah's time find in the solemni-
ties of the passover, who, when they had
kept seven days according to the law,
in attending on God's ordinances, " took
counsel together to keep other seven
days, and they kept other seven days
with gladness." And if Christ's hearers
had not found an abundant sweetness
and satisfaction in attending on him,
they could never have continued their
attendance those days in a desert place,
as we find they did, Matt. xv. 32. No
wonder then that his own disciples,

when they were spectators of his trans-figuration, and auditors of his discourse with Moses and Elias in the holy mount, said, " Master, it is good to be here ;" here let us make tabernacles.

3. They will say that they have found the pleasure of religion sufficient to over-come the pains and troubles of sense. and to take out the sting of them, and take out the terror of them. This is a plain evidence of the excellency of spiritual pleasures, that religious convictions will soon conquer sensual delights, and quite extinguish them ; so that they become as " songs to a heavy heart," for a " wounded spirit who can bear ?" But it has often been found, that the pains of sense have not been able to extinguish spiritual delights, but have been con-quered and quite overbalanced by them. Joy in spirit has been to many a power-ful alloy to trouble in the flesh.

The pleasure that holy souls have in God, as it needs not to be supported by the delights of sense, so it fears not being suppressed by the grievances of sense. They can rejoice in the Lord, and joy in him as the God of their salvation, even then, when the "fig-tree doth not blossom, and there is no fruit in the vine,' for even then, when in the world they have tribulation, Christ hath provided that in him they should have satisfaction.

For this we may appeal to the martyrs, and other sufferers for the name of Christ. How have their spiritual joys made their bonds for Christ easy, and made their prisons " delectable orchards," as one of the martyrs called his. Animated by these comforts, they have not only taken patiently, but " taken joyfully the spoiling of their goods, knowing in themselves that they have in heaven a better, and a more enduring substance." Ask Paul, and he will tell you, that even then, when he was " troubled on every side," when without were fightings, and within were fears, yet he was filled with comfort, and was exceeding joyful in all his tribulations, and that as his sufferings for Christ increased, his consolation increased proportionably. And though he expects no other but to finish his course

with blood, yet he doubts not but
to finish his course with joy. Nay,
we may appeal to the sick-beds and
death-beds of many good Christians for proof of this. When wearisome nights have been appointed to
them, yet God's " statutes have been
their songs in the night. " I have pain,"
says one, " but I bless God I have peace."
" Weak and dying," said another, " but
light and comfort enough within." The
delights of sense forsake us, when we
most need them to be a comfort to us.
When a man is " chastened with pain
upon his bed, and the multitude of his
bones with strong pain, he abhorreth
bread and dainty meat," and cannot
relish it ; but then the bread of life and
spiritual dainties have the sweetest relish
of all. Many of God's people have found
it so : " This is my comfort in mine affliction, that thy word hath quickened
me." This has " made all their bed in
their sickness," and made it easy.

4. They have found, that the closer
they have kept to religion's ways, and
the better progress they have made in

those ways, the more pleasure they have found in them. By this it appears, that the pleasure takes its excellency from the religion—the more religion prevails, the greater the pleasure is. What disquiet and discomfort Wisdom's children have, is owing, not to Wisdom's ways —those are pleasant—but to their deviations from those ways, or their slothfulness and trifling in them. These things are indeed unpleasant, and sooner or later will be found so. If good people are sometimes drooping and in sorrow, it is not because they are good, but because they are not so good as they should be. They do not live up to their profession and principles, but are too much in love with the body, and hanker too much after the world. Though they do not turn back to Sodom, they look back towards it, and are too mindful of the country from which they came out ; and this makes them uneasy ; this forfeits their comforts and grieves their Comforter, and disturbs their peace, which would have been firm to them, if they had been firm to their engagements. If we turn aside out of the ways of God, we are not to think it strange if the consolations of God do not follow us. But "if we cleave to the Lord with full purpose of heart," then we find the "joy of the Lord our strength." Have we not found those duties most pleasant, in which we have taken most pains and most care? have we not had the most comfortable Sabbath-visits made to our souls when we have been most "in the Spirit on the Lord's day?" And the longer we continue and the more we mend our pace in these ways, the more pleasure we find in them. This is the excellency of spiritual pleasures, and recommends them greatly that they increase with use, so far they are from withering or going to decay. The difficulties which may at first be found in the ways of religion wear off by degrees, and the work of it grows more easy, and the joys of it more sweet.

Ask those who have backslidden from the ways of God, have left their first love, and, begin to bethink themselves and to remember whence they are fallen, whether they had not a great deal more comfort when they kept close to God, than they have had since they turned aside from him; and they will say with that adultress, when she found the way of her apostacy hedged up with thorns, " I will go and return to my first husband, for then it was better than with me now." There is nothing got by departing from God, and nothing lost by being faithful to him.

CHAPTER V.

THE DOCTRINE ILLUSTRATED BY THE SI-
MILITUDE USED IN THE TEXT, OF A
PLEASANT WAY OR JOURNEY.

THE practice of religion is often spoken of in scripture as a way. It is the way of God's commandments; it is a highway, the King's highway, the King of kings' highway; and those that are religious are travelling in this way. The schoolmen commonly called Christians in this world, Viatores—travellers; when they come to heaven, they are Comprehensores—they have then attained, are at home. Here they are on their journey, there at their journey's end. Now if heaven be the journey's end, " the

prize of our high calling," and we be
sure, if we so run as we ought, that we
shall obtain, it is enough to engage and
encourage us in our way, though it be
ever so unpleasant ; but we are told
that we have also a pleasant road.

Now there are ten things which help
to make a journey pleasant, and there is
something like to each of these to be
found in the way of Wisdom, by those
that walk in that way.

I. It helps to make a journey pleasant to go upon a good errand. He that
is brought up a prisoner in the hands of
the ministers of justice, whatever conveniences he may be accommodated with,
cannot have a pleasant journey, but a
melancholy one ; and that is the case of
a wicked man. He is going on this
world towards destruction : the way he
is in, though wide and broad, leads directly to it ; and while he persists in it,
every step he takes is so much nearer
hell, and therefore he cannot have a
pleasant journey ; it is absurd and in-
decent to pretend to make it so. Though
the way may seem right to a man, yet

there can be no true pleasure in it, while the end thereof is the ways of death, and the "steps take hold on hell."

But he that goes into a far country to receive for himself a kingdom, whatever difficulties may attend his journey, yet the errand he goes on is enough to make it pleasant; and on this errand they go that travel Wisdom's ways. They look for a kingdom which cannot be moved, and are pressing forward in the hopes of it. Abraham went out of his own country, " not knowing whither he went;" but those that set out and hold on in the way of religion, know whither it will bring them; they know that it leads to life, eternal life ; and therefore, " in the way of righteousness is life," because there is such a life at the end of it.

Good people go upon a good errand, for they go on God's errand as well as their own. They are serving and glorifying him, contributing something to his honour, and the advancement of the interests of his kingdom among men ; and this makes it pleasant. And that which puts so great a reputation upon the duties of religion, that by them God is served and glorified, cannot but put so much the more satisfaction into them. With what pleasure does Paul appeal to God, as the God whom " he served with his spirit in the gospel of his Son !"

II. It helps to make a journey pleasant, to have strength and ability for it. He that is weak, sickly, and lame, can find no pleasure in the pleasantest walks. How should he, when he takes every step in pain! A strong man rejoices to run a race, but he that is feeble trembles to set one foot before another. Now this makes the ways of religion pleasant, that they who walk in those ways, are not only cured of their natural weakness, but are filled with spiritual strength ; they travel not in their own might, but in the " greatness of his strength," who is " mighty to save." Were they to proceed in their own strength, they would have little pleasure in the journey. Every little difficulty would foil them, and they would tire

presently ; but they go forth, and go on
in the strength of the Lord God ; and
npon every occasion, according to his
promise, he renews that strength to them,
and they "mount up with wings like
eagles," they go on with cheerfulness and
alacrity ; " they run, and are not weary ;
they walk, and do not faint." God,
with his comforts, enlarges their hearts,
and then they not only go, but "run in
the way of his commandments."

That which to the old nature is im-
practicable and unpleasant, and which
therefore is declined, or undertaken with
reluctancy, to the new nature is easy
and pleasant : and this new nature is
given to all the saints, and puts a new
life and vigour into them, strengthens
them with all might in the inner man,
unto all diligence in doing-work, patience in suffering-work, and persever-
ance in both ; and so all is made pleasant. They are "strong in the Lord,
and in the power of his might," and this
not only keeps the spirit willing, even
when the flesh is weak, but makes even

the "lame man to leap as an hart, and the tongue of the dumb to sing."

III. It helps to make a journey pleasant to have a good guide, whose knowledge and faithfulness one can confide in. A traveller, though he has daylight, yet may miss his way, and lose himself, if he have not one to show him his way and go before him, especially if his way lie, as ours does, through a wilderness where there are so many by-paths: and though he should not be guilty of any fatal mistake, yet he is in continual doubt and fear, which makes his journey uncomfortable. But this is both the safety and the satisfaction of all true Christians, that they have not only the gospel of Christ for their light, as a discovering and directing light, but the Spirit of Christ for their guide. It is promised, that he shall "lead them into all truth," shall "guide them with his eye." Hence they are said to "walk after the Spirit," and to be "led by the Spirit," as God's Israel of old were led through the wilderness by a pillar of cloud and fire, and the Lord was in it.

IV. It helps to make a journey pleasant, to be under a good guard or convoy, that one may travel safely. Our way lies through an enemy's country, and they are active, subtle enemies. The road is infested with robbers, who lie in wait to spoil, and to destroy. We travel by the lions' dens, and the mountains of the leopards; and our danger is the greater, because it arises, not from flesh and blood, but spiritual wickedness. Satan, by the world and the flesh, way-lays us, and seeks to devour us, so that we could not with any pleasure go on our way, if God himself had not taken us under his special protection. The same Spirit that is a guide to these travellers, is their guard also; for whoever are sanctified by the Holy Ghost, are by him "preserved in Christ Jesus blameless;" and shall be preserved to the heavenly kingdom, so that they shall not be robbed of their graces and comforts, which are evidences for, and earnests of eternal life. They are "kept by the power of God, through faith unto salvation," and therefore may go on

cheerfully. The promises of God are
a writ of protection to all Christ's good
subjects in their travels, and give them
such a holy security, as lays a foundation for a constant serenity. Eternal
truth itself has assured them, that no
evil shall befall them, nothing really
and destructively evil, no evil but what
God will bring good to them out of.
God himself has engaged to be their
keeper, and to preserve their going out
and coming in, from henceforth and for
ever, which promise looks as far for-
wards as eternity itself: and by such
promises as these, and that grace which
is conveyed through them to all active
believers, God carries them as upon
eagles' wings, to bring them to himself.

Good angels are appointed for a guard
to all that walk in Wisdom's ways, to
bear them in their arms, where they go,
and to pitch their tents round about them
where they rest, and so to keep them in
all their ways. How easy may they
be that are thus guarded, and how well
pleased under all events! as Jacob was,

who " went on his way, and the angels of God met him."

V. It helps to make a journey pleasant, to have the way tracked by those that have gone before in the same road, and on the same errand. Untrodden paths are unpleasant ones; but in the ways of religion, we are both directed and encouraged by the good examples of those that have chosen the way of truth before us, and have walked in it. We are bidden to follow them, who are now " through faith and patience," those travelling graces of a Christian, " inheriting the promises."

It is pleasant to think that we are walking in the same way with Abraham, and Isaac, and Jacob, with whom we hope shortly to sit down in the kingdom of God. How many holy, wise, good men, have governed themselves by the same rules that we govern ourselves by, have lived with the same views and by the same faith that we live by, looking for the same blessed hope ; and have by it " obtained a good report !" We " go forth by the footsteps of the flock."

Let us therefore, to make our way easy and pleasant, take the prophets for an example. And "being compassed about with so great a cloud of witnesses, let us run with patience and cheerfulness, the race that is set before us, looking unto Jesus," the most encouraging pattern of all, who has "left us an example, that we should follow his steps;" and what more pleasant than to follow such a leader, whose word of command is, "Follow me?"

VI. It helps to make a journey pleasant to have good company. This deceives the time, and takes off the tediousness of a journey as much as any thing. It is the comfort of those who walk in Wisdom's ways, that though there are but few walking in those ways, yet there are some, and those the wisest and best, and more excellent than their neighbours; and it will be found there are more ready to say, "we will go with you, for we have heard that God is with you."

The communion of saints contributes much to the pleasantness of Wisdom's ways. We have many fellow-travellers that quicken one another, by the fellow-ship they have one with another, as companions in the kingdom and patience of Jesus Christ. It was a pleasure to those who were going up to Jerusalem to worship, that their numbers increased in every town they came to, and so they " went from strength to strength ;" they grew more and more numerous, " till every one of them in Zion appeared before God ;" and so it is with God's spiritual Israel, to which we have the pleasure of seeing daily additions of such as shall be saved.

VII. It helps to make a journey pleasant, to have the way lie through green pastures, and by the still waters ; and so the ways of Wisdom do. David speaks his experience herein, that he was led into the " green pastures," the verdure whereof was grateful to the eye, and " by the still waters," whose soft and gentle murmurs were music to the ear : and he was not driven through these, but made to lie down in the midst of these delights, as Israel when they encamped at Elim, where there were twelve wells of water, and threescore and ten palm trees. Gospel-ordinances, in which we deal much in our way to heaven, are as agreeable to all the children of God, as these green pastures and still waters. They call the Sabbath a delight, and prayer a delight, and the word of God a delight. These are their pleasant things. There "is a river" of comfort in gospel ordinances, "the streams whereof make glad the city of God, the holy place of the tabernacles of the Most High;" and along the banks of this river their road lies.

Those that turn aside from the ways of God's commandments are upbraided with the folly of it, as leaving a pleasant road for an unpleasant one. Will a man, a traveller, be such a fool as to leave the fields, which are smooth and even, for a rock that is rugged and dangerous, or for the snowy mountains of Lebanon? Shall the running waters be forsaken for the strange cold waters? Thus are men enemies to themselves, and the foolishness of man perverteth his way.

VIII. It adds to the pleasure of a journey to have it fair over-head. Wet and stormy weather takes off very much of the pleasure of a journey; but it is pleasant travelling when the sky is clear, and the air calm and serene: and this is the happiness of those who walk in Wisdom's ways, that all is clear between them and heaven; there are no clouds of guilt to interpose between them and the Sun of Righteousness, and to intercept his refreshing beams; no storms of wrath gathering, that threaten them. Our reconciliation to God, and acceptance with him, makes every thing pleasant. How can we be melancholy, if heaven smile upon us? "Being justified by faith, we have peace with God," and peace from God, peace made for us, and peace spoken to us, and then "we rejoice in tribulation." Those travellers cannot but rejoice all the day, who "walk in the light of God's countenance."

IX. It adds likewise to the pleasure

of a journey, to be furnished with all
needful accommodations for travelling.
They that walk in the way of God,
have wherewithal to bear their charges,.
and it is promised them that they shall
want no good thing.   If they have not
an abundance of the wealth of this world,
which perhaps does but overload a traveller, and prove an incumbrance rather
than any furtherance, yet they have
good bills; having access by prayer to
the throne of grace wherever they are,
and a promise that they shall receive
what they ask; and access by faith to
the covenant of grace, which they may
draw upon, and draw from, as an inex-
haustible treasury.   "Jehovah Jireh;
the Lord will provide."

X. It helps to make a journey pleasant to have a good prospect.   The travellers in Wisdom's ways may look
about them with pleasure, so as no travellers ever could : for they can call all
about them their own, even the " world,
and life and death, and things present
and things to come ; all is theirs, if they
be Christ's."   The whole creation is not

only at peace with them, but at their service.

It is pleasant in a journey, to have a prospect of the journey's end; to see that the way we are in leads directly to it, and to see that it cannot be far off, nay, that we are within a few steps of it. We have a prospect of being shortly with Christ in paradise. Yet a little while, and we shall be at home, we shall be at rest; and whatever difficulties we may meet with in our way, when we come to heaven, all will be well, eternally well.

CHAPTER VI.

THE DOCTRINE VINDICATED.

" Suffer me a little," says Elihu to
Job, " and I will show thee that I have
yet to speak on God's behalf," something
more to say in defence of this truth,
against that which may seem to weaken
the force of it. We all ought to concern ourselves for the vindication of godliness, and to speak what we can for it,
for we know that it is every where
spoken against. There is no truth so
plain, so evident, but there have been
those who have objected against it. The
prince of darkness will raise what mists
he can to cloud a truth, that stands so

directly against his interest; but great is the truth, and will prevail.

Now, as to the truth of the pleasantness of religion—

I. It is easy to confront the reproaches of the enemies of religion, who give it an ill name. There are those who make it their business, having perverted their own ways, to pervert the right ways of the Lord, and to cast an odium upon them; as Elymas the sorcerer did, with a design "to turn away the deputy from the faith." They are like the wicked spies, that brought up an evil report of the promised land, as a land that did eat up the inhabitants thereof; and neither could be conquered, nor was worth conquering.

Now, in answer to these calumnies we have this to say, that the matter is not so. They who say thus of religion, "speak evil of the things which they know not." The devil, we know, was a liar from the beginning, and a false accuser of God and religion; and represented God to our first parents as having dealt hardly and unjustly with them,

in prohibiting them the " tree of knowledge ;" as if he envied them the happiness and pleasure they would at-
tain to by eating of that tree ; and the
same method he still makes use of to
alienate men's minds from the life of
God and the power of godliness. But
we know and are sure, that it is a ground-
less imputation, for Wisdom's ways are
" ways of pleasantness, and all her paths
are peace."

II. It is easy also to set aside the
misrepresentations of religion, which are
made by some that call themselves its
friends, and profess kindness for it. As
there are enemies of the Lord that blas-
pheme, so there are among the people of
the Lord those that give them great occasion to do so, as David did. How
many wounds does religion receive in
the house of her friends ! false friends
they are, or foolish ones ; unworthy to
be called Wisdom's children, for they
do not justify her as they ought ; but
through mistake and indulgence of their
own weakness, betray her cause instead
of pleading it and witnessing to it ; and

confirm people's prejudices against it, which they should endeavour to remove.

Some that profess religion are morose and sour in their profession, peevish and ill-humoured, and make the exercises of religion a burden and task, and a terror to themselves and all about them ; while it ought to sweeten the spirit, and make it easy, and candid, and compassionate to the infirmities of the weak and feeble of the flock.

Others are melancholy and sorrowful in their profession, and go mourning from day to day under prevailing doubts and fears, and disquietudes about their spiritual state. We know some of the best of God's servants have experienced trouble of mind to a great degree.

As to the former, it is their sin ; and let them bear their own burden, but let not religion be blamed for it : and as to the latter, though there are some very good people that are of a sorrowful spirit, yet we will abide by it, that true piety has true pleasure in it notwithstanding. But God is sometimes pleased, for wise and holy ends, to suspend for a time the communication of his comforts to his people, and to hide his face from them, to try their faith, that it may be "found to praise, and honour, and glory, at the appearing of Christ," and so much the more for their being a while " in heaviness through manifold temptations." Thus he corrects them for what has been done amiss by them, and takes this course to mortify what is amiss in them. Even winter seasons contribute to the fruitfulness of the earth. Thus he brings them to a closer and more humble dependence upon Christ for all their comfort, and teaches them to live entirely upon him. And though " for a small moment he thus forsakes them," it is but to magnify his power so much the more in supporting them, and to make his returns the sweeter, for he will gather them with " everlasting loving-kindness." Light is sown for them, and it will come up again.

As this is their affliction, God's hand must be acknowledged in it, his righteous hand ; yet there is sin in it ; and that is from themselves. Good people have not the comforts they might have in their religion, and whose fault is it? They may thank themselves; they run themselves into the dark, and shut their eyes against the light. " My wounds stink and are corrupt," says David. " The wounds of sin which I gave myself are unhealed, not bound up, or mollified with ointment." And why? Is it for want of balm in Gilead, or a physician there? No; he owns it is because of his foolishness; he did not take the right method with them. God speaks joy and gladness to his people, but they turn a deaf ear to it, like Israel in Egypt, that hearkened not to Moses, for "anguish of spirit, and for cruel bondage." But let not the blame be laid upon religion, which has provided comfort for their souls, but let them bear the blame whose souls refuse to be comforted, or who do not take the way appointed for comfort. David owns that the reason why he wanted comfort, and was in pain, and agitated, was because he " kept silence." He was not so free with God as he might and should have been; but when he said, " I will confess my transgressions unto the Lord," he was forgiven, and all was well.   Psalm xxxii. 3, 5.

Those do both God and Christ, and themselves and others, a deal of wrong, who look upon him with whom they have to do in religion, as one that seeks an occasion against them and counts them for his enemies, and is extreme to mark what they think, or say, or do amiss; whereas he is quite otherwise, is slow to anger, swift to mercy, and willing to make the best of those whose hearts are upright with him, though they are com- passed about with infirmity.   He will not always chide ; he does not delight in the " death of them that die," but would rather that they should " turn and live."   Nor does he delight in the tears of them that weep, does not "afflict willingly, nor grieve the children of men," much less his own children ; but would rather they should be upon good grounds comforted.   Religion then clears itself from all blame, which some may take occasion to cast upon it, from the uncomfortable lives which some lead that are religious.

III. But it will require more pains to reconcile this truth of the pleasantness of religious ways, with that which the word of God itself tells us of, the difficulties with which the ways of Religion are attended. We value not the misapprehensions of some, and the misrepresentations of others, concerning religious ways: but we are sure the word of God is of a piece with itself, and does not contradict itself. Our Master has taught us to call the way to heaven a narrow way, that is, an afflicted way, a distressed way; and we have in Scripture many things that declare it to be such. But this does not contradict the doctrine, that the ways of Wisdom are pleasant; for the pleasantness that is in Wisdom's ways is intended to be a balance, and is very much an overbalance, to any thing in them which is any way distasteful or incommodious. As for the imaginary difficulties which the sluggard dreams of, " a lion in the street," we do not regard them; but there are some real difficulties in it, as well as real comforts. "God hath set the one over-against the other," that we might study to comport with both, and might sing, and sing unto God of both. We will not, we dare not, make the matter better than it is, but will allow there is that in religion which at first view may seem unpleasant; and yet doubt not but to shew that it is reconcileable to, and consistent with, all that pleasure which we maintain to be in religion, and so to take off all exceptions against this doctrine.

There are four things which seem not well to agree with this doctrine, and yet it is certain they do.

1. It is true, that to be religious is to live a life of repentance, and yet religious ways are pleasant notwithstanding. It is true, that we must mourn for sin daily, and reflect with regret upon our manifold infirmities; sin must be bitter to us, and we must even loathe and abhor ourselves for the corruptions which dwell in us, and the many actual trans-

gressions which are committed by us.
We must renew our repentance daily,
and every night must make some sorrowful reflections upon the transgressions of
the day. But then it is not walking in
the way of Wisdom that creates us this
sorrow, but our trifling in that way, and
our turning aside out of it. If we would
keep close to these ways, and pass forward in them as we ought, there would
be no occasion for repentance. If we
were as we should be, we should be always praising God, and rejoicing in him;
but we make other work for ourselves
by our own folly, and then complain
that religion is unpleasant; and whose
fault is that? If we would be always
loving and delighting in God, and would
live a life of communion with him, we
should have no occasion to repent of
that; but if we leave the fountain of
living waters, and turn aside to broken
cisterns, or the brooks in summer, and
see cause to repent of it, we may thank
ourselves. What there is of bitterness
in repentance, is owing not to our religion, but to our defects and defaults in

religion ; and it proves that there is
bitterness, not in the ways of God, but
in the ways of sin, which makes a peni-
tential sorrow necessary, for the pre-
venting of a sorrow a thousand times
worse ; for sooner or later sin will have
sorrow.   If repentance be bitter, we
must not say, this is occasioned through
being godly, but through being sinful.
" This is thy wickedness, because it is
bitter."   If by sin we have made sorrow necessary, it is certainly better to
mourn now than " to mourn at the
last."   To continue impenitent, is not
to put away sorrow from thy heart,
but to put it off to a worse place.

Even in repentance, if it be right, there
is a true pleasure, a pleasure accompany-
ing it.   Our Saviour has said of them
who thus mourn, not only that " they
shall be comforted," but that they " are
blessed."   When a man is conscious to
himself that he has done an ill thing,
and what is unbecoming him and may
be hurtful to him, it is incident to him
to repent of it.   Now religion has found
a way to put a sweetness into that bit-

terness. Repentance, when it is not from the influence of religion, is nothing but bitterness and horror, as Judas's was; but repentance, as it is made an act of religion, as it is one of the laws of Christ, is pleasant, because it is the raising of the spirit, and the discharging of that which is noxious and offensive. Our religion has not only taken care that penitents be not overwhelmed with an excess of sorrow, and swallowed up by it, that their sorrow do not work death, as the sorrow of the world does; but it has provided that even this bitter cup should be sweetened; and therefore we find that, under the law, the sacrifices for sin were commonly attended with expressions of joy: and while the priests were sprinkling the blood of the sacrifices to make atonement, the Levites attended with psalteries and harps, for so was the commandment of the Lord by his prophets. Even the day to afflict the soul is the day of atonement; and when we receive the atonement, we "joy in God through our Lord Jesus Christ." In giving our consent to the atonement, we take the comfort of the atonement. In sorrowing for the death of some dear. friend or relation, thus far we have found a pleasure in it, that it has given vent to our grief which our spirits were full of : so in sorrow for sin, the shedding of just tears is some satisfaction to us. The same word in Hebrew signifies both to comfort and to repent, because there is comfort in true repentance.

Much more after repentance, there is a pleasure flowing from it. It is a way of pleasantness, for it is the way to pleasantness. To them that · mourn in Zion, that sorrow after a godly sort, God hath appointed " beauty for ashes, and the oil of joy for mourning." And the more the soul is humbled under the sense of sin, the more sensible will the comfort of pardon be ; it is wounded in order to be healed. The Jubilee trumpet sounded in the close of the day of soul-affliction, which proclaimed the acceptable year of the Lord, the year of release.

2. It is true, that to be religious is to take care, and to take pains, and to labour earnestly ; and yet Wisdom's ways

are " ways of pleasantness." It is true,
we must strive to enter into this way ;
must be in agony, so the word is. There
is a violence which the kingdom of
heaven suffers, and the " violent take it
by force !" The bread of life is to be
eaten in the sweat of our face. We
must be always upon our guard, and
keep our hearts with all diligence.
Business for God and our souls is what
we are not allowed to be slothful in,
but we are to be " fervent in spirit, serving the Lord." We are " soldiers of
Jesus Christ," and we must endure hard-
ness, must war the good warfare till it
be accomplished.

And yet even in this contention, there
is comfort. It is work indeed, and work
that requires care ; and yet it will appear to be pleasant work, if we consider
how we are strengthened for it, and animated with strength in our souls to go
on in it, and go through with it. It
would be unpleasant, and would go on
very heavily, if we were left to ourselves, to travel in our own strength ;
but if we be actuated and animated in

it by a better spirit and mightier power
than our own, it is pleasant. If God
work "in us both to will and to do of
his good pleasure," we shall have no reason to complain of the difficulty of our
work; for God "ordains peace for us,"
true peace and pleasure, by working all
our works in us. It is observable that
when God, though he eased not Paul of
the thorn in the flesh, yet said that good
word to him, " My grace is sufficient
for thee," immediately it follows,
" Therefore I take pleasure in infirmities, in reproaches, in distresses for
Christ's sake; for when I am weak,
then I am strong." Sufficient grace
will make our work pleasant, even the
hardest part of it. It will appear to be
pleasant work, if we consider how we
are encouraged in it. It is true, we
must take pains, but the work is a good
work, and is to be done, and is done by
all the saints, from a principle of holy
love, and that makes it pleasant; as
Jacob's service for Rachel was pleasant
to him, because he loved her. It is an
unspeakable comfort to industrious Chris-

tians, that they are working together with God and he with them; that their master's eye is upon them and a witness to their sincerity; that "he sees in secret," and will "reward openly." God now accepts their works, smiles upon them, and his Spirit speaks to them good words, and "comfortable words," witnessing to their adoption. And this is very encouraging to God's servants, as it was to the servants of Boaz to have their master come to them, when they were hard at work, reaping down his own fields, and with a pleasant countenance say to them, "The Lord be with you." Nay, the Spirit says more to God's labourers,—"the Lord is with you."

The prospect of the recompence of reward, is in a special manner encouraging to us in our work, and makes it pleasant, and the difficulties we meet with in it to be as nothing. It was by giving an eye to this that Moses was encouraged, not only to bear the reproach of Christ, but to "esteem it greater riches than the treasures of Egypt." In all labour there is profit, and if so, there is pleasure also in the prospect of that profit, and according to the degree of it. We must work, but it is to work out our salvation, a great salvation, which, when it comes, will abundantly make us amends for all our toil. We must strive, but it is to enter into life, eternal life. We must run, but it is for an incorruptible crown, the prize of our high calling. And we do not run at any uncertainty, nor fight as those that beat the air; for to him that "sows righteousness there is a sure reward," and the assurance* of that harvest will make even the seed-time pleasant.

3. It is true, that to be religious is to deny ourselves in many things that are pleasing to sense ; and yet Wisdom's ways are pleasantness notwithstanding. It is indeed necessary that beloved lusts should be mortified and subdued, corrupt appetites crossed and displeased, which to the natural man is like "plucking out a right eye, and cutting off a right hand." There are forbidden pleasures that must be abandoned, and kept at a distance

from : the flesh must not be gratified, nor " provision made to fulfil the lusts of it," but on the contrary, we must " keep under the body, and bring it into subjection;" we must " crucify the flesh," must kill it, and put it to a painful death. The first lesson we are to learn in the school of Christ, is to deny ourselves, and this must be our constant practice : we must use ourselves to deny ourselves, and thus " take up our cross daily."

Now, will not this spoil all the pleasure of a religious life ? No ; it will not; for the pleasures of sense, which we are to deny ourselves, are comparatively despicable and really dangerous.

These pleasures we are to deny ourselves, are comparatively despicable. How much soever they are valued and esteemed by those who live by sense, and know no better, they are looked upon with a generous contempt by those who live by faith, and are acquainted with divine and spiritual pleasures. And it is no pain to deny ourselves in these pleasures, when we know ourselves entitled to better, more rational, and noble, and agreeable, the delights of the blessed spirits above. When a man has learned to put a due estimate upon spiritual pleasures, those that are sensual have lost all their sweetness, and are become the most insipid things in the world; he has no pleasure in them, in comparison with that far greater pleasure which excelleth. Is it any diminution to the pleasure of a grown man, to deny himself the toys and sports which he was fond of when a child? No; when he becomes a man, he puts away these childish things. He is now past them, he is above them, for he is acquainted with those entertainments that are manly and more generous. Thus mean and little do the pleasures of sense appear to those that have learned to delight themselves in the Lord.

They are really dangerous; they are apt to take away the heart. If the heart be set upon them, they blind the mind, debauch the understanding and conscience, and in many quench the sparks of conviction, and of that holy fire which comes from heaven, and tends to heaven. They are in danger of drawing away the heart from God, and the more they are valued and coveted, the more dangerous they are, the more likely to pierce us through with many sorrows, and to drown us in destruction and perdition. To deny ourselves in them, is but to avoid a rock, upon which multitudes have fatally split.

What diminution is it to the pleasure of a safe and happy way on sure ground, which will certainly bring us to our journey's end, and to deny ourselves the false and pretended satisfaction of walking in a fair but dangerous way, that leads to destruction? Is it not much pleasanter travelling on a rough pavement, than in a smooth quicksand? Where there is a known peril, there can be no true pleasure, and therefore the want of it is no loss or uneasiness.

What pleasure can a wise or considerate man take in those entertainments, in which he has continual reason to suspect a snare and a design upon him, any more than he that was at a feast could relish the dainties of it, when he was aware of a naked sword hanging over him by a single thread? The foolish woman indeed calls the "stolen waters sweet, and bread eaten in secret pleasant;" but those find no difficulty or uneasiness in denying them, who know "that the dead are there, and her guests are already in the depths of hell."

4. It is true, that "through much tribulation we must enter into the kingdom of God;" that we must not only deny ourselves the pleasures of sense, but must sometimes expose ourselves to its pains; that we must take up our cross when it lies in our way, and bear it after Christ. We are told, that "all that will live godly in Christ Jesus must suffer persecution," at least they must expect it, and get ready for it; bonds and afflictions abide them; losses in their estates, hindrances in their preferment, reproaches and contempts, banishments, deaths, must be counted upon, and will not this spoil the pleasure of religion? No, it will not; for it is but "light affliction" at the worst, that we are called to suffer and "but for a moment," com-

pared with the " far more exceeding and eternal weight of glory" that is reserved for us, with which the" sufferings of this present time are not worthy to be compared." All these troubles do but touch the body, the outward man, and the interests of it ; they do not at all affect the soul. They break the shell, or pluck off the husk, but do not bruise the kernel.

Can the brave and courageous soldier take pleasure in the toils and perils of the camp, and in jeoparding his life in the high places of the field, in the eager pursuit of honour, and in the service of his prince and country ? and shall not those who have the interest of Christ's kingdom near their hearts, and are carried on by a holy ambition of the honour that comes from God, take a delight in suffering for Christ, when they know that those sufferings tend to his honour, and their own hereafter ? They that are " persecuted for righteousness' sake, that are reviled, and have all manner of evil said against them falsely, because they belong to Christ, are bidden not only to bear it patiently, but to rejoice in it, and to be " exceeding glad, for great is their reward in heaven." Every reproach we endure for Christ, will be a pearl in our crown shortly.

As those afflictions abound for Christ, so our " consolations in Christ do much more abound." The more the waters increased, the higher was the ark lifted up. The more we suffer in God's cause, the more we partake of his comforts ; for he will not be wanting to those whom he calls out to any extraordinary hardships for his name's sake. Thus the extraordinary supports and joys which they experience who patiently suffer for righteousness' sake, add much more to the pleasantness of the ways of Wisdom, than the sufferings themselves do or can derogate from it ; for the sufferings are human, the consolations are divine. They suffer in the flesh, but they rejoice in the spirit ; they suffer for a time, but they rejoice evermore; and "this their joy no man taketh from them."

CHAPTER VII.

THE APPLICATION OF THE DOCTRINE.

CONCERNING this doctrine of the pleasantness of religious ways, I hope we may now say, as Eliphaz does of his principle, " Lo! this we have searched it ; so it is ;" it is incontestibly true, and therefore we may conclude as he does, " Hear it, and know thou it for thy good ;" know thou it for thyself, so the margin reads it ; apply it to thyself, believe it concerning thyself, not only that it is good, but that " it is good for thee to draw near to God." Then only we hear things, and know them for our good.

when we hear them and know them for ourselves.

The inferences, by way of counsel and exhortation, we shall draw from this doctrine.—

1. Let us all be persuaded and prevailed with to enter into and to walk in these paths of wisdom that are so very pleasant.

Is a life of religion such a sweet and comfortable life? Why then should not we be religious? If such as these be the ways of Wisdom, why should not we be travellers in those ways? Let this recommend to us a life of sincere and serious godliness, and engage us to conform to all its rules, and give up ourselves to be ruled by them. It is not enough to have a good opinion of religion, and to give it a good word; that will but be a witness against us, if we do not set ourselves in good earnest to the practice of it, and make conscience of living up to it.

I would here, with a particular and pressing importunity, address myself to you that are young, to persuade you, now in the days of your youth, now in the present day, to make religion your choice and your business ; and I assure you, if you do so, you will find it your delight. That which I would persuade you to, is to walk in the ways of Wisdom, to be sober-minded, to be thoughtful about your souls and your everlasting state, and to get your minds well-principled, and well-affected, and well-inclined. " Wisdom is the principal thing, therefore get wisdom, and with all thy getting get understanding." That of which I would persuade you, is the pleasantness of this way; you cannot do better for yourselves than by a religious course of life.

I wish you would see and seriously consider, the two rivals that are making court to you for your souls, for your best affections, Christ and Satan ; and act wisely in disposing of yourselves, and make such a choice as you will afterwards reflect upon with comfort. You are now at the turning time of life ; turn right now, and you are made for ever. Wisdom says, " Whoso is sim ple, let him turn in" to me; and she will cure him of his simplicity. Folly says, " Whoso is simple, let him turn in" to me; and she will take advantage of his simplicity. Now let him come, whose right your hearts are, and give them him, and you shall have them again more your own.

That you may determine well between these two competitors for the throne in your souls, see, first, the folly of carnal sinful pleasures, and abandon them : you will never be in love with the pleasures of religion till you are persuaded to fall out with forbidden pleasures. The enjoyments of the delights of sense suit best with the age of youth; the appetite towards them is then most violent; mirth, sport, plays, dainties, are the idols of young people, they are therefore called " youthful lusts." The days will come, the evil days, when they themselves will say they have " no pleasure in them," like Barzillai, who, when he was old, can no more relish what he eats and what he drinks. Oh that reason, and wisdom, and grace, might make you as dead to them now, as time and days will make you after a while!

Will you believe one that tried the utmost of what the pleasures of sense could do towards making a man happy? He said of laughter, " It is mad," and of mirth, " What doth it ?" and that " sorrow is better than laughter." Moses knew what the pleasures of a court were, and yet chose rather to suffer affliction with the people of God, than to continue in the snare of them; and you must make the same choice ; for you will never cordially embrace the pleasures of religion, till you have renounced the pleasures of sin. Covenant against them therefore, and watch against them.

Look upon sinful pleasures as mean and much below you ; look upon them as vile and much against you ; and do not only despise them, but dread them, and " hate even the garments spotted with the flesh."

Secondly, Be convinced of the pleasure of Wisdom's ways, and come and try them. You are, it may be, prejudiced against religion as a melancholy thing, but, as Philip said to Nathanael, " Come and see." Believe it possible that there may be a pleasure in religion which you have not yet thought of. When religion is looked upon at a distance, we see not that pleasure in it, which we shall certainly find when we come to be better acquainted with it. Come, and take Christ's yoke upon you, and you will find it easy. Try the pleasure there is in the knowledge of God and Jesus Christ, and in converse with spiritual and eternal things; try the pleasure of seriousness and self-denial, and you will find it far exceeds that of vanity and self-indulgence. Try the pleasure of meditation on the word of God, of prayer, and praise, and sabbath-sanctification, and you will think that you have made a happy change of the pleasure of vain and carnal mirth for these true delights.

Make this trial by these four rules— First, That man's chief end is to glorify God, and enjoy him. Our pleasures will be according to that which we pitch upon and pursue as our chief end. If we can mistake so far as to think it is our chief end to enjoy the world and the flesh, and our chief business to serve them, the delights of the sense will relish best with us : but if the world was made for man, certainly man was made for more than the world ; and if God made man, certainly he made him for himself. God then is our chief good, it is our business to serve and please him, and our happiness to be accepted of him.

Secondly, That the soul is the man, and that is best for us, which is best for our souls. Learn to think meanly of the flesh, by which we are allied to the earth and the inferior creatures. It is formed out of the dust, it is dust, and it is hastening to the dust ; and then the things that gratify it, will not be esteemed of any great moment. " Meats for the belly, and the belly for meats ; but God shall destroy both it and them ;" and therefore let us not make idols of them. But the soul is the noble part of us, by which we are allied to heaven, and the world of spirits. Those comforts therefore which delight the soul, are the comforts we should prize most, and give the preference to, for the soul's sake. Rational pleasures are the best for a man.

Thirdly, That the greatest joy is that which a stranger doth not intermeddle with. The best pleasure is that which lies not under the eye and observation of the world, but which a man has, and hides in his own bosom, and by which he enjoys himself, and keeps not only a peaceable, but a comfortable possession of his own soul; though he does not by laughter, or other expressions of joy, tell them the satisfaction he has. Christ had "meat to eat which the world knew not of," and so have Christians, to whom he is the bread of life.

Fourthly, That all is well that ends everlastingly well. That pleasure ought to have the preference, which is of the longest continuance. The pleasures of sense are withering and fading, and leave a sting behind them to those that place their happiness in them; but the pleasures of religion will abide with us; "in these is continuance;" they will not

turn with the wind, nor change with the
weather, but are meat which endures to
everlasting life. Reckon that the best
pleasure, which will remain with you,
and stand you in stead when you come
to die; which will help to take off the
terror of death, and allay its pains. The
remembrance of sinful pleasures will
give us killing terrors, but the remembrance of religious pleasures will give
us living comforts in dying moments.

II. Let us who profess religion, study
to make it more and more pleasant to
ourselves. We see how much is done
to make it so; let us not receive the
grace of God herein in vain. Let them
that walk in wisdom's ways, taste the
sweetness of them, and relish it. Christ's
service is perfect freedom; let us not
make a drudgery of it, nor a toil of such
a pleasure. We should not only be reconciled to our duty, as we ought to be
to our greatest afflictions, and to make
the best of it, but we should rejoice in
our duty, and sing at our work. If God
intended that his service should be a
pleasure to his servants. let them concur

with him herein, and not walk contrary
to him.

Now, in order to the making of our
religion increasingly pleasant to us, I
shall give seven directions.

1. Let us always keep up good
thoughts of God, and carefully watch
against hard thoughts of him.   As it is
the original error of many that are loose
and careless in religion, that they "think
God altogether such an one as themselves," as much a friend to sin as themselves, and as indifferent whether his
work be done or not; so it is the error
of many who are severe in their religion,
that they think God, like themselves, a
hard Master. They have such thoughts
of him, as Job had in an hour of temptation, when he looked upon God as
seeking occasions against him, and taking him for his enemy; as if he were
extreme to mark iniquities, and impla-
cable to those who had offended, and
not accepting any service that had in it
the least defect or imperfection. But
the matter is not so; and we do both
God and ourselves a great deal of wrong,

if we imagine it to be so. What could have been done more than God has done, to convince us that he is gracious, and merciful, " slow to anger," and ready to forgive sin when it is repented of? Let us deal with him accordingly. Let us look upon God as love, and the God of love, and then it will be pleasant to us to hear from him, to speak to him, to converse with him, and to do him any service.

It is true, God is great, and glorious, and jealous, and to be worshipped with reverence and holy fear; but is he not our Father, a tender, gracious Father? Was not God, in Christ, " reconciling the world to himself," and to all his attributes and relations to us, by showing himself willing to be reconciled to us, notwithstanding our provocations? See him, therefore, upon a throne of grace, and come boldly to him, and that will make your service pleasant.

2. Let us dwell much by faith upon the promises of God. What pleasant lives should we lead, if we were but more intimately acquainted with those

declarations which God has made of his
good will to man, and the assurances he
has given of his favour and all the blessed fruits of it, to those who serve him
faithfully ?   The promises are many and
exceeding great and precious, suited to
our case, and accommodated to every
exigence ; there are not only promises to
grace, but promises of grace, grace sufficient ; and these promises are all " yea
and amen in Christ."   And what do
these promises stand in our Bibles for,
but to be made use of ? Come then, and
let us apply them to ourselves, and in-
sert our own names in them by faith.
What God said to Abraham, " I am thy
shield," I am ' El-shaddi, a God all-sufficient,'—what he said to Joshua, " I
will never fail thee nor forsake thee," he
says to me.   What he says to all that
love him, that " all things shall work
for good to them," and to all that " fear
him," that " no good thing" shall be
wanting to them, he says to me ; and
why should not I take the comfort of
it ?

3. Let us order the affairs of our re-

ligion with discretion. Many make religion unpleasant to themselves and dis-
couraging to others, by their imprudent
management of it; making that service
to be a burden by the circumstances of
it, which in itself would be a pleasure;
doing things out of time, or tasking
themselves above their strength, and undertaking more than they can go through
with, especially at first, which is like
"putting new wine into old bottles," or
like "overdriving the flocks." If we make
the yoke of Christ heavier than he has
made it, we may thank ourselves that
our drawing in it becomes unpleasant.
But let us take our religion as Christ
has settled it, and we shall find it easy.
When the ways of our religion are ways
of wisdom, then they are ways of pleasantness; for the more wisdom the more
pleasantness. 'Wisdom dwells with
prudence.' Wisdom will direct us to
be even and regular in our religion, to
take care that the duties of our general
and particular calling, the business of
our religion and our necessary business
in the world, do not interfere or intrench

upon one another. It will direct us to
time duty aright; for every thing is
beautiful and pleasant in its season, and
work is then easy when we are in the
frame for it.

4. Let us live in love, and keep up
Christian charity, and the spiritual communion of saints. If we would be of
good comfort, we must be of one mind,
and therefore the apostle presses brother-
ly love upon us, with an argument taken
from the consolations in Christ, Phil ii.
1, that is, the comfort that is in Christianity. As ever you hope to have the
comfort of your religion, submit to that
great law of it, "Walk in love;" for
"Behold, how good and how pleasant
it is, for brethren to dwell together in
unity." The more pleasing we are to
our brethren, the more pleasant we
shall be to ourselves.

Nothing makes our lives more uncomfortable than strife and contention;
"Woe is me that I dwell among those
that hate peace." It is bad being among
those that are disposed to quarrel, and
worse, having in ourselves a disposition

to quarrel. The resentments of contempt put upon us, are uneasy enough, and contrivances to revenge it are much more so. And nothing makes our religion more uncomfortable, than strifes and contentions about it. We forfeit and lose the pleasure of it, if we entangle ourselves in perverse disputings about it. But by holy love we enjoy our friends, which will add to the pleasure of enjoying God in this world. Love itself sweetens the soul, and revives it, and, as it is the loadstone of love, it fetches in the further pleasure and satisfaction of being beloved, and so it is a heaven upon earth; for what is the happiness and pleasure of heaven, but that there love reigns in perfection? Then we have most peace in our bosoms, when we are most peaceably disposed towards our brethren.

5. Let us be much in the exercise of holy joy, and employ ourselves much in praise. Joy is the heart of praise, as praise is the language of joy. Let us engage ourselves to these, and quicken ourselves in them. God has made these

our duty, that by these all the other parts of our duty may be pleasant to us; and for that end we should abound much in them, and attend upon God with joy and praise. Let us not crowd our spiritual joys into a corner of our hearts, nor our thankful praises into a corner of our prayers, but give both scope and vent to both.

Let us be frequent and large in our thanksgivings. It will be pleasant to us to recount the favours of God, and thus to make some returns for them; though poor and mean, yet such as God will graciously accept. We should have more pleasure in our religion, if we had but learned in " every thing to give thanks," for this takes out more than half the bitterness of our afflictions, that we can see cause even to be thankful for them; and it infuses more than a double sweetness into our enjoyments, that they furnish us with matter for this excellent heavenly work of praise. " Sing praises unto his name, for it is pleasant;" comfortable, as well as comely.

Let us live a life of delight in God, and love to think of him as we do of one whom we love and value. Let the flowing in of every stream of comfort lead us to the fountain ; and in every thing that is grateful to us, let us taste that the Lord is gracious. Let the drying up of every stream of comfort drive us to the fountain; and let us rejoice the more in God for our being deprived of that which we used to rejoice in.

6. Let us act in a constant dependence upon Jesus Christ. Religion would be much more pleasant, if we did but cleave more closely to Christ in it, and do all in his name. The more precious Christ is to us, the more pleasant will every part of our work be; and therefore believing in Christ is often expressed by our rejoicing in him. We may rejoice in God, through Christ, as the Mediator between us and God ; may rejoice in our communion with God, when it is kept up through Christ ; may rejoice in hope of eternal life, when we see this life in the Son. "He that hath

the Son of God, has life, that is, he has comfort."

There is that in Christ, and in his undertaking and performances for us, which is sufficient to satisfy all our doubts, to silence all our fears, and to balance all our sorrows. He was appointed to be " the Consolation of Israel," and he will be so to us, when we have learned not to look for that in ourselves, which is to be had in him only, and to make use of his mediation in every thing wherein we have to do with God. When we rejoice in the righteousness of Christ, and in his grace and strength ; when we rejoice in his satisfaction and intercession, in his dominion and universal agency and influence, and in the progress of his gospel, and the conversion of souls to him, and please ourselves with prospects of his second coming, we have then a joy, not only which no man takes from us, but which will increase more and more ; and of the increase of Christ's government, and therefore of that peace, there shall be no end. Our songs of joy are then most pleasant, when the bur-

den of them is, ' None but Christ ; none
but Christ.'

7. Let us converse much with the
glory that is to be revealed. They
that by faith send their hearts and best
affections before them to heaven, while
they are here on this earth, may in return fetch thence some of those joys and
pleasures that are at God's right hand.
That which goes up in vapours of holy
desire, though insensible, in groanings
which cannot be uttered, will come down
again in dews of heavenly consolations,
which will make the soul as a watered
garden.

Let us look much to the end of our
way, how glorious it will be, and that
will help to make our way pleasant.
This abundantly satisfies the saints, and
is the fatness of God's house on earth.
This makes them now to " drink of the
river of God's pleasures," that " with
him is the fountain of life," whence all
these streams come, and "in his light
they hope to see light," everlasting light.
By frequent meditations on that rest
which remains for the people of God, we

M

now enter into that rest, and partake of the comfort of it.

Our hopes of that happiness through grace would be very much strengthened, and our evidences for it cleared up insensibly, if we did but converse more with it, and the discoveries made of it in the scripture. We may have foretastes of heavenly delights, while we are here on earth, clusters from Canaan, while we are yet in this wilderness, and there is no pleasure comparable to that which these afford. That is the sweetest joy within us, which is borrowed from the joy set before us. And we deprive ourselves very much of the comfort of our religion, in not having our eye more to that joy. We rejoice most triumphantly, and with the greatest degrees of holy glorifying, when we " rejoice in hope of the glory of God." In this " our heart is glad, and our glory rejoices."

III. Let us make it appear, that we have indeed found wisdom's way to be pleasantness, and her paths peace. If we have experienced this truth, let us evidence our experience ; and not only in word, but in deed, bear our testimony to the truth of it. Let us live as those who believe the sweetness of religion, not because we are told it, but because we have tasted it.

If so be then, we " have tasted that the Lord is gracious ;" if we have, indeed, found it a pleasant thing to be religious—

1. Let our hearts be much enlarged in all religious exercises, and all instances of gospel-obedience. The more pleasant the service of God is, the more we should abound in it. When God enlarges our hearts with his consolations, he expects that we should run the way of his commandments, that we should exert ourselves in our duty with more vigour, and press forward the more earnestly towards perfection.

What is really our delight, we are no soon weary of. If we delight in ap proaching to God, we shall seek him daily, and make it our daily work to honour him. If meditation and prayer be sweet, let them be our daily exercise ;

and let this bind our souls with a bond
to God, and the "sacrifice as with cords
to the horns of the altar." With this
we should answer all temptations to a-
postacy—' Shall I quit so good a Master, so good a service ? Entreat me not
to leave Christ, or to turn from follow-
ing after him ; for it is good to be here.'
" Here let us make tabernacles." Whither else shall we go, but to him that
has the words of eternal life ?

2. Let our whole conversation be
cheerful, and melancholy be banished.
Are the ways of religion pleasant? Let
us be pleasant in them, both to ourselves,
and to those about us. As for those who
are yet in a state of sin and wrath, they
have reason to be melancholy ; let the
sinners in Zion be afraid, be afflicted, joy
is forbidden fruit to them ; what have
they to do with peace ? " Rejoice not,
O Israel, for joy, as other people, for
thou hast gone a-whoring from thy
God." But those, who, through grace,
are called out of darkness into marvellous light, have cause to be cheerful, and
should have hearts to be so. " Arise,

shine, for thy light is come." Is the Sun
of Righteousness risen upon us? Let us
arise and look forth as the morning
with the morning. That comfort which
Christ directs to our souls, let us reflect back upon others. And as our
light is come, so is our liberty. Art
thou "loosed from the bands of thy neck,
O captive daughter of Zion? Awake,
awake, awake, put on thy strength, put
on thy beautiful garment, and shake
thyself from the dust."

Though vain and carnal mirth is both
a great sin and a great snare, yet there
is a holy cheerfulness and pleasantness
of conversation, which will not only con-
sist very well with serious godliness,
but greatly promote it in ourselves, and
greatly adorn it, and recommend it to
others. "A merry heart," Solomon says,
" doeth good like a medicine, and makes
fat the bones; while a broken spirit does
hurt like a poison, and dries the bones."
Christians should endeavour to keep up
a cheerful temper, and not indulge
themselves in that which is saddening
and disquieting to the spirit and they

should show it in all holy conversation,
that those they converse with, may see
they did not renounce pleasure, when
they embraced religion.

Are we in prosperity? Let us therefore be cheerful, in gratitude to the God
of our mercies, who expects that we
should "serve him with joyfulness and
gladness of heart, in the abundance of
all things," and justly takes it ill if we
do not. Are we in affliction? Yet let
us be cheerful, that we may make it
appear that our happiness is not laid up
in the creature, nor our treasures on
earth. If it is the privilege of Christians to rejoice in tribulations, let them
not throw away their privilege, but glory
in it, and make use of it. Let the joy
of the Lord, which has infused itself into our hearts, diffuse itself into all our
converse. "Go thy way, eat thy bread
with joy, and drink thy wine;" nay,
if thou shouldest be reduced to drink
mere water, drink it "with a merry
heart," if thou hast good ground to hope
that in Christ Jesus, God now accepts
thy works; and this joy of the Lord
will be thy strength.

3. Let us look with contempt upon
the pleasures of sense, and with abhor-
rence upon the pleasures of sin. The
more we have tasted of the delights of
heaven, the more our mouths should be
put out of taste with the delights of
this earth. Let not those who have
been feasted with the milk and honey
of Canaan, hanker after the garlic and
onions of Egypt.

Let us keep at a distance from all
forbidden pleasures. There is a hook
under those baits; a snake under that
green grass; a rock under those smooth
waters, on which multitudes have split.
Either spiritual pleasures will deaden
the force of the pleasure of sin, or
the pleasures of sin will spoil the relish
of spiritual pleasures. Let us keep up
a holy indifference even to the lawful
delights of sense, and take heed not to
love them more than God. The eye
that has looked at the sun, is dazzled to
every thing else. Have we beheld the
beauty of the Lord? Let us see, and
own how little beauty there is in other
things. If we be tempted to do any

thing unbecoming us by the allurements of pleasure, we may well say, 'Offer these things to those that know no better; but we will never leave fountains of living water for cisterns of puddle water.'

4. Let not our hearts envy sinners. Envy arises from an opinion that the state of others is better than our own, which we grudge and are displeased at, and wish ourselves in their condition. Good people are often cautioned against this sin; "Be not thou envious against evil men, nor desire to be with them;" for if there be all this pleasure in religion, and we have experienced it, surely we would not exchange our condition with any sinner even in his best estate.

Envy not sinners their outward prosperity, their wealth and abundance. Envy not sinners the liberty they take to sin; that they can allow themselves in the full enjoyment of those pleasures which we cannot think of without horror. Have not we the enjoyment of pleasures which are infinitely better, and which they are strangers to ? We cannot have both ; and of the two, are not ours, without dispute, preferable to theirs ; and why then should we envy them ? Their pleasures are enslaving, ours enlarging ; theirs debasing to the soul, ours enno- bling ; theirs surfeiting, ours satisfying ; theirs offensive to God, ours pleasing to him ; theirs will end in pain and bitter- ness, ours will be perfected in endless joys ; what reason then have we to envy them ?

5. Let not our spirits sink or be de- jected under the afflictions of this present time. We disparage our comforts in God, if we lay too much to heart our crosses in the world; and therefore hereby let us evince, that being satisfied of God's loving kindness, we are satis- fied with it. Let us look upon that as sufficient to balance all the unkindness- es of men. They that value themselves upon God's smiles, ought not to vex themselves at the world's frowns. The light of God's countenance can shine through the thickest clouds of the trou- bles of this present time : and therefore

we should walk in the light of the Lord,
even when, as to our outward condition,
we sit in darkness.

6. Let the pleasure we have found in
religion, dispose us to be liberal and
charitable to the poor and distressed.
The pleasing sense we have of God's
bounty to us, by which he has done so
much to make us easy, should engage
us bountifully to distribute to the neces-
sities of saints, according to our ability,
not only to keep them from perishing,
but to make them easy, and that they
may rejoice as well as we. Cheerfulness
that enlarges the heart, should open the
hand too. Paul observes it concerning
the churches of Macedonia, who were
ready to give for the relief of the poor
saints at Jerusalem, that it was the
" abundance of their joy," their spiritual joy, their joy in God, that " abound-
ed unto the riches of their liberality."
When the people of Israel are commanded to " rejoice in every good
thing" which God had given them, they
are commanded also to give freely to
" the Levite, the stranger, the fatherless,

and the widow, that they may eat, and be filled." And when, upon a particular occasion, they are directed to "eat the fat, and drink the sweet," Neh. viii. 10, at the same time they are directed to "send portions unto them for whom nothing is prepared;" and then the joy of the Lord will be their strength. By our being charitable, we should show that we are cheerful; that we cheerfully taste God's goodness in what we have, and trust his goodness for what we may hereafter want.

7. Let us do what we can to bring others to partake of the same pleasures in religion which we have tasted, especially those who are under our charge. It adds very much to the pleasure of an enjoyment, to communicate of it to others, especially when the nature of it is such, that we have never the less, but the more rather, for others sharing in it. What good tidings we hear that are of common concern, we desire that others may hear and be glad too. He that has but found a lost sheep, calls his friends and neighbours to re-

joice with him; but he that has found Christ, and found comfort in him, can say, not only, 'Come, rejoice with me,' but, 'Come and partake with me;' for yet there is room enough for all, though ever so numerous; enough for each, though ever so necessitous and craving.

8. Let us be willing to die, and leave this world. We have reason to be ashamed of ourselves, that we, who have not only laid up our treasures above, but fetch our pleasures thence, are as much in love with our present state, and as loath to think of quitting it, as if our riches, and pleasure, and all, were wrapt up in the things of sense and time. The delights of sense entangle us and hold us here. These are the things that make us loath to die, as one once said, viewing his fine house and gardens. And are these things sufficient to court our stay here, when God says, " Arise, and depart, for this is not your rest?"

Let us not be afraid to remove from a world of sense to a world of spirits, since we have found the pleasures of sense not worthy to be compared with spiritual pleasures. When in old age, which is one of the valleys of the shadow of death, we can no longer relish the delights of the body, but they become sapless and tasteless, as they were to Barzillai, yet we need not call those " evil days," and " years in which we have no pleasure," if we have walked and persevered in wisdom's ways; for if so, we may then in old age look back with pleasure upon a life well spent on earth, as Hezekiah did, and look forward with more pleasure, upon a life to be better spent in heaven. And when we have received a sentence of death within ourselves, and see the day approaching, the pleasure we have in loving God and believing in Christ, and in the expressions of holy joy and thankfulness, should make even a sick-bed and a death-bed easy. ' The saints shall be joyful in glory, and shall sing aloud upon their beds,' those beds to which they are confined, and from which they are removing to their graves, their beds in the darkness. Our religion, if we be faithful to it, will furnish us with living comforts in dying moments, sufficient to balance the pains of death, and take off the terror of it, and to enable us to triumph over it; " O death, where is thy sting ?" Let us then evidence our experience of the pleasures of religion, by living above the inordinate love of life, and fear of death.

9. Let us long for the perfection of these spiritual pleasures in the kingdom of glory. When we come thither, and not till then, they will be perfected. While we are here, as we know and love but in part, so we rejoice but in part. Even our spiritual joys here, have their damps and alloys; we mix tears and tremblings with them; but, in heaven, there is a " fulness of joy without mixture," and " pleasures for evermore," without period or diminution. The servants of Christ will there enter into the joy of their Lord, and it shall be " everlasting joy."

And what are the pleasures in the way of wisdom, compared with those at the end of the way ? If a complacency in the divine beauty and love be so pleasant while we are in the body, and are absent from the Lord, what will it be when we have put off the body, and go to be present with the Lord? If a day in God's courts, and a few minutes spent there in his praises, be so pleasant; what will an eternity within the veil be among them that dwell in his house above, and are still praising him? If the earnest of our inheritance be so comfortable, what will the inheritance be? Now wherever there is grace, it will be aiming at and pressing towards its own perfection. It is a "well of water springing up to eternal life." · This therefore we should be longing for. Our love to God in this world is love in motion, in heaven it will be love at rest: O when shall that sabbatism come, which remains for the people of God? Here we have the pleasure of looking towards God : "O when shall we come and appear before him?" Our Lord Jesus, when at his last passover, which he earnestly desired to eat with his disciples, had tasted of the "fruit of the vine," speaks as one that longed to drink it new in the kingdom of his Father. It is very pleasant to serve Christ here, but to "depart and be with Christ, is far better." "Now are we the sons of God," and it is very pleasant to think of it: but "it doth not yet appear what we shall be." Something there is in reserve, which we are kept in expectation of. We are not yet at home, but we should long to be there, and keep up holy desires of that glory to be revealed, that we may be quickened, as long as we are here, to press "toward the mark for the prize of the high calling."

FINIS.